Dwayne's Guitar Lessons Presents:

Learn To Play Electric Guitar

By

Dwayne Jenkins

Introduction

The electric guitar was invented out of necessity. By many different people as far back as the 1920's. The need to make the then acoustic guitar louder. This was thought to be done through means of electricity and amplification.

The goal was to develop, design, and popularize a much louder instrument. This was needed to keep up with the volume of playing with drummers and other instruments that could get louder naturally through playing them. This could only be done by figuring out a way to control the volume.

An acoustic guitar can only get so loud no matter how hard you play it. Unlike a trumpet, saxophone or drum set. So the next step was inevitable. Figure out a way to make the guitar louder. This would allow guitar players to compete in volume.

With bigger musical ensembles and concert halls filling up, musicians needed to be louder. One of the reasons the Beatles stopped touring, is they couldn't hear themselves over all the screaming girls. But then again, not a bad problem to have huh?

Anyway, this volume control became possible by using new materials and designs. First there was the amplified acoustic guitar and then came the solid bodied electric guitar. A new idea that would revolutionize the music industry.

When it comes to solid bodied electric guitars, there are two names we think of in this modern world. Although there were many in its development, the two most popular are Mr. Les Paul, and Mr. Leo Fender.

These two men did for electric guitar, what Henry Ford did for automobiles. Especially Leo Fender. Not only did he develop electric guitar amplifiers, but he also invented the most iconic electric guitar in the world. The Fender Stratocaster.

Now I don't want to go on and on about the electric guitar as that could be a book all its own, but the idea of learning how to play it sounds like a whole lot of fun to me. And that my friend, is what this book is all about.

So if you're ready, let's dive in and look at what it takes to learn to play the electric guitar. In doing so, you will not only develop new skill sets and an appreciation for this wonderful invention, but you will also develop confidence within yourself.

Dwayne Jenkins

Table of Contents

Introduction

Chapter 1 Getting Started

Lesson 1: Electric guitar parts

When it comes to getting started playing electric guitar nothing fancy is needed. Although I recommend you start with a quality entry level guitar or a pre-owned upgraded version of one. This will make learning easier and allow you to progress faster.

An electric guitar is very similar to an acoustic guitar, as far as some of the guitar parts, but where they differ is in the solid body. This allows for easier pickup installation & creativity options in body shapes and styles.

Once you find that guitar you really like, it motivates you to practice. That's why it's a good idea to get familiar with the guitar itself. All the parts of the guitar, how they function, and how you can use that to boost your inspiration.

The more you know about the guitar and how it works, the more appreciation you'll begin to develop for this wonderful instrument. The guitar is the best instrument in the whole musical instrument family, and it is for this reason I choose to teach it.

So let's look at the electric guitar and get familiar with the parts:

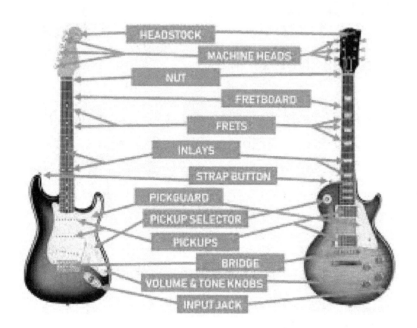

In the picture above we have the two most common types of electric guitars. The Fender Strat, and the Gibson Les Paul. So I will use these as a guideline. Although they are designed a bit differently, they are built very similar.

Headstock: This is the top of the guitar where the machine heads are located.

Machine Heads: These are what hold the strings on and get the guitar in tune.

Nut: This is what holds the guitar strings in place so that you can form chords.

Fretboard: This is the top of the guitar neck. It is where you will form and play your chords and scales.

Frets: The metal wires that separate the fretboard into playing positions.

Inlays: These are dots that represent where you are on the fretboard.

Strap Button: Where you apply a strap for playing standing up.

Pick Guard: This keeps the body of the guitar from getting scratched by the guitar pick when strumming chords.

Pickup Selector: This is what allows you to select different pickups for more tone diversity.

Pickups: These are what allow the electric guitar to be amplified and thus volume controlled to be louder.

Bridge: This is where the strings are held in place on the body of the guitar.

Volume & Tone Knobs: These are what allow you to control the volume & type of guitar tone.

Output Jack: This is for the cable that goes to the amplifier or effects pedals. This allows for more volume & tone options.

Almost all electric guitars are built like this with these features. It is such features as the pickups and output jack that allow the electric guitar to sound the way we know it today. They are what allow us to enhance the guitar tone with pedals.

We will get into guitar pedals a bit later in the training, but for now we want to just get familiar with the guitar itself. The more you know about your instrument and the components associated with it (amplifier included) the more you'll be able to get out of it.

Pickups are very important because they produce different sounds for the guitar. In the Fender style guitar you have single coil pickups that produce a clear, crisp sound great for playing both rhythm & lead.

The Les Paul style guitar uses what's known as humbuckers. Basically two single coil pickups together that produce a fatter more chunkier sound than single coil pickups. These can also be great for playing rhythm and lead guitar.

Both of these are great choices and provide a wide variety of guitar creativity for a number of different styles of music. The single coil pickups work great for certain styles and the dual coil (humbuckers) work great for others.

Some guitars out there have a combination of both single & dual pickups in them. These give you the best of both worlds. So that might be an option to consider as well. Just make sure it is of at least entry level quality if not better.

Depending on your style of musical inspiration, you want to choose the one that fits accordingly. Most guitar players eventually get both. Kind of like an apple and an orange. Similar fruits, but also very different.

Lesson 2: Learning guitar posture

When it comes to playing the guitar you can do it in two positions, sitting down or standing up. For our purposes here I recommend you learn the instrument sitting down. Later you can work at playing it standing up.

The electric guitar (acoustic also) is designed specifically for this purpose. To feel comfortable when playing it sitting down. The body shape is curved in such a way that you can play it sitting down and be comfortable.

This is how the electric guitar was originally played when it was just a backup instrument. As the years went by and the guitar started to get the spotlight, people started standing up to play it. This allowed for more radical guitar shapes to be created.

No matter if you sit down or stand up, you want to make sure the guitar feels comfortable. Sitting down, it should rest on your leg like the picture below.

If you choose to stand up to play it while you learn, that's ok too. You just need to get you a guitar strap so that the guitar can hang comfortably when you play it. This will hook on two ends of the guitar like the picture below.

When playing the guitar standing up, you want to make sure that the guitar is well balanced. So some adjustment might need to be made. But ultimately it should look something like this:

If you choose to play standing up, get a good guitar strap.

Lesson 3: Positioning of both hands

Playing the guitar is a combination of both mental and physical activity. Especially the hands. One hand is doing one thing, while the other is doing something completely different. This is what can make the instrument a bit challenging at first.

But not to worry, this method book will make learning to play the electric guitar as easy as possible. That way you'll spend more time learning and playing, and less time scratching your head trying to figure it all out.

One hand will be your fretboard hand where you will learn to form guitar chords and switch between them. Your other hand will be your picking hand where you will learn to create rhythm and melody. By strumming and picking the strings.

Your fretboard hand

With this hand you will form and play the guitar chords. These will be the foundation for the song progression. Development of this hand is crucial and will take time.

Here is a good example of how your hand should look.

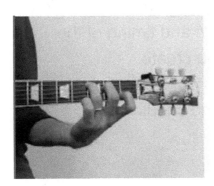

In the picture you can see how a chord is formed (this is the C major chord) and this will require some discipline to get it right. But then that is what makes it an accomplishment.

You want your thumb to be facing up in the back (never have it facing down) as this will help you to push the strings on the fretboard and hold the chords down.

Your fingers will be placed on the front on the fretboard and form chords along multiple strings. As well as switch between them once you learn to form the chords properly.

It will take some time to develop your hand and finger muscles as they are not used to being in this position. So be patient when learning. It will come if you stick with it and know, all great guitar players started here.

Your picking hand

The development of this hand is vitally important as well. This hand is what's going to create the rhythm and timing of the chord progressions and melody lines you create.

Here is a good example of how your hand should look.

Everyone plays a bit different and as you progress with the training, you will find what works best for you. I recommend as a guideline that you start out with keeping your hand close to the strings.

You will also be playing with a guitar pick which will allow you to execute these techniques more effectively. I'll get into how to use that in later lessons.

When it comes to your picking hand, you want to keep your wrist loose for strumming. You might also want to anchor your pinky and ring finger to the guitar body. This will help for hand stability when arpeggiating guitar chords.

Your wrists should be loose and comfortable. Make sure when you strum or pick the strings individually you do it right over the pickups. These pickup the vibration of the strings and send it to the amplifier to be heard.

How your hands approach the guitar will make a difference on how well you execute certain techniques. As you get better you'll discover what works best. Use what I teach as a starting point for your hand positioning development.

Now that we know about the electric guitar, how to hold it and roughly what each of our hands are supposed to do, let's look at how to get it tuned up so we can start playing it.

Lesson 4: Tuning up the guitar

The thing that is most important when playing the electric guitar (or any instrument for that matter) is making sure that it is in tune. Without this learned skill of knowing how to tune the guitar, all your efforts will be wasted. And we don't want that!

So we must learn how to get the guitar in tune and keep it in tune. The best way to do so is with an electronic tuner. These are very handy, inexpensive and easy to use.

Now before we can tune the guitar with one of these tuners (there are many to choose from) we need to learn the names of our strings. This tells us what to tune the guitar strings to.

All six strings from low E to high E.

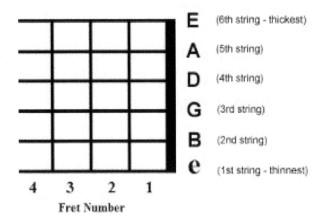

E (6th string - thickest)

A (5th string)

D (4th string)

G (3rd string)

B (2nd string)

e (1st string - thinnest)

4   3   2   1
Fret Number

One way of remembering the string names is to use an acronym like:

Eddie
Ate
Dynamite
Good
Bye
Eddie

This simple phrase will help you to remember the string names for tuning the guitar. This will also help in learning your guitar notes. Which we will go over later in the training.

Another way to help remember the strings is to figure your smallest string is the 1st string smallest number, and your biggest string is the 6th string biggest number. The acronym and number system will make learning the strings easier.

Once we have this all figured out, we can look at some guitar tuners. Since there are many to choose from, we'll take a look at a few and get the guitar tuned up. Then we can get to the fun part. Learning how to play the instrument.

Clip-on tuners

These are the most popular guitar tuners. They are small and just clip on to the headstock of your guitar (remember what the headstock is?) then give you a reading based off of the vibration of the strings.

These are very easy to use. They provide a nice big display of the note so that it can be seen very easily, can be placed in multiple positions and come in many different colors to match your guitar.

They run on a simple watch battery. They can be stored in your guitar case, or left on your guitar ready for action at a moment's notice.   These guitar tuners can be found online or at your favorite local music store.

Guitartuna app.

Here is another great tuner that works well. And since it's an app, it will be with you wherever you go because it'll be on your phone. This gives you the convenience of having a tuner on hand at all times.

This tuner works the same way as the clip-on tuner. From the vibration of your strings. You merely find it in the app store, download it for free and open up the app. It's available for both android & iphone.

Simple, nice display and easy to use. Plus it has additional learning functions. Like a metronome and learning guitar chord games that you don't get with the clip-on tuner. Not to mention that it's free and no battery needed.

Pitch fork and Tuning pipes

A pitch fork produces a single pitch when struck and you tune one string to that pitch. Then you tune the rest of the strings accordingly.

Tuning pipes provide a pitch for all six strings. You blow into the pipe to produce the pitch and then tune the string to that pitch.

These are not as commonly used today for guitar playing as all tuning has gone electronic. But these can be great for ear training. For now, I recommend that you just use the clip-on tuner or app. It will get you going much faster.

Lesson 5: Using a guitar pick

The most common way to bring to life these techniques we've discussed so far, is with a guitar pick. A simple little plectrum you hold in your picking hand as you strum or strike the guitar strings.

The guitar pick is a guitarist's best friend. Although you can play without one as many people do, I recommend you start out learning to use one. It helps get the most out of an amplified electric guitar.

Before we can learn to strum chords, create rhythms, or play melody lines, we must learn about the guitar pick. How to hold it and how to get the most benefit from using it.

As you can see from this picture, guitar picks come in many different shapes and sizes. They also come in different colors, thickness and materials. This is great for you because you can find one that matches your style and personality.

I recommend you go to your local music store or shop online and get a few different ones to try out. You can buy a pack of assortment picks for this specific purpose.

Also make sure to get picks made of quality by companies such as Fender, Dunlop, Gibson, or Ernie Ball. I personally prefer Dunlop guitar picks.

Dunlop makes a variety of guitar picks that are useful for both electric and acoustic and have been making guitar picks for many years. So I'm sure with enough research, you'll find the guitar pick that works best for you.

Holding the guitar pick

Now that we have found the ultimate guitar pick we want to use, we must learn how to hold it in our hand. The pictures below will give a good example of this.

Everyone plays a bit different and that's ok. But I recommend you use these pictures as a guideline to get started.

You place the pick between your thumb and first finger with your fingers curved in like the picture shows. Then you place your thumb over the top to hold it in place.

Once you have the pick you want, practice holding it properly. This is very important as proper pick placement will allow you to get the most out of the guitar strings.

Using a guitar pick has many advantages:

1. Helps to produce a clear defined tone
2. Increases the volume considerably
3. Helps with strumming and arpeggiating chords
4. Increases speed for quick melody lines

This and many more things are beneficial when using a guitar pick on an electric guitar. So don't overlook this lesson. It will serve you well into the future of your guitar playing.

Chapter 1 Summary

In this first chapter we have covered some basics of the electric guitar. This will set the foundation for all your future studies. From this book and other books you will learn from in the future.

First we have the electric guitar itself. An amazing invention really. And as time goes on, you will become more aware of this. To really learn the instrument it is best to know the instrument well.

Know its parts. What they are, how they function and how they work in harmony with each other to create the overall sound of the instrument. This will help you to develop a much greater appreciation for it.

Second we learn the proper posture to hold the guitar. This is very important as it can make a huge difference on getting the most out of the guitar as you learn to play it. Knowing how to hold it will allow you to play it for hours with comfort.

This will keep you motivated and inspired to learn. As concepts and techniques get easier to understand and apply, you will see how the time will pass with ease. This is when you'll know you're having fun.

<u>Third</u> we have our hand positioning. This is also very important as it will determine how well we actually play the instrument. If you take the proper time to develop these skills, you will sound amazing.

You will be able to make the guitar sound like music that people want to listen to. Plus you won't experience as much fatigue and wrist strain with proper hand positioning.

<u>Fourth</u> we look at the most important concept of them all, tuning the guitar. Without learning this, anything we decide to play will sound terrible. You'll have people covering their ears running for safety.

No matter if we have the other three concepts down to a tee, you need to learn this lesson well. It will make all the difference in your playing.

<u>Fifth</u> we have the guitar pick. Learn how to hold and use this. It will become your best friend when it comes to playing the guitar. Just make sure you try out a few different ones to get what works best for you.

This will allow you to produce a cleaner clearer tone, increase your volume of chords and melodies and allow you to increase your speed for those hot-rockin guitar solos. If you so choose to play them.

22

Chapter 2 Electric guitar Amplifier

Lesson 6: Types of amplifiers

Before we learn how to play the guitar we want to learn about another very important component. The electric guitar amplifier. This is what makes this wonderful invention possible. It allows for volume control.

Like I stated before, there was a need for guitars to be louder. By the introduction of a few things like electricity, pickups, and amplification, this was now possible. The ability to make the guitar louder and more noticeable.

Let's look at some amplifier examples:

Not only did Leo Fender create the most iconic guitar on the market, he also created guitar amplifiers. Here we have a combo amp. This is where the amp and speaker are in one unit. Easy to play, and easy to transport.

Another example, is where the amp and speaker unit are seperate. Like in the Marshall half stack:

This kind of amplifier is more for stage use. Although they do make some that are smaller so you can practice with them at home. But basically the amp is seperate from the speaker to allow more diversity in tone when using different speakers.

Amplifiers come in basically two types. Solid state and tube. You now also have a hybrid of both in some cases, but mostly they will fall into one of these two catagories. Kind of like an apple and an orange. Similar but different.

As you learn about amplifiers more on your journey of learning to play electric guitar, you'll find what one works best for your needs. They both have their pros and cons and depending on what you like the sound of, will determine what amp you choose

Solid state amplifiers

This type of amp uses transistor circuits to convert an electric signal into an audio sound wave. It is this signal conversion that allows the vibration of the strings that flow through the pickups in the electric guitar to be heard through the amp & speaker.

Solid state amps are very popular because they are less expensive, they are lighter in weight, less maintenance, and they allow for on-board effects to help enhance your guitar playing creativity. These are very popular for beginners.

Tube or valve amplifiers

The other type of amplifier is the tube amp, or valve amp as it is sometimes called. This type of amplifier uses vacuum tubes to increase the power of the guitar signal. As well as push it to the point where it breaks up and distorts.

Tube amps provide a much warmer natural tone than solid state amplifiers. This is because they are voltage regulated and not transistor regulated. These types of amps are also usually much heavier due to the tubes and transformers in them.

Both of these types of amps work roughly in the same way. With two stages. A pre-amp stage and a power stage. The guitar signal comes into the amp, is boosted by the preamp stage and then boosted again by the power stage.

This is what allows you to control the volume of an electric guitar and why an amplifier is needed. Unlike an acoustic guitar where the sound hole produces the volume.

I recommend you go to your local music store and try both types out. Listen for the difference and see which one suits you best. Both amps will do the job when it comes to learning and playing the electric guitar.

Since tube amps are more expensive, I'd say start on a solid-state amp. But if you prefer the sound of the tube amp, then I recommend you save up some money and get that one instead.

A benefit that both styles of amplifiers have is the ability to control and shape the guitar signal. This is done with options that are very similar to a radio. This is what allows you to have a lot of fun playing electric guitar.

Amplifiers are neat in the fact that they allow you to not only control the volume, but also shape your guitar tone.

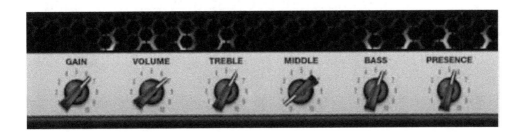

As you can see there are knobs on the amp that allow you to control the volume, treble, bass, etc. Very much like a home stereo.

Here is another example of guitar signal modification. As you can see here, you have many options to create your own sound. This will enhance your learning experience and fuel your inspiration.

Lesson 7: Guitar cables

Guitar cables are very important because they carry the signal from the guitar to the amplifier. They also are important if you decide to use effects pedals. Which we will discuss in the next lesson. But for now let's focus on the cables.

This is a traditional kind of guitar cable. A ¼ inch jack on each end. One for the guitar and one for the amplifier. The cable comes out of the output jack on the guitar and plugs into the input jack of the amplifier.

Like the guitar and the amplifier, you have many options to choose from. Different types, lengths, and colors. Here are a few more options.

Here is a nice yellow cable that looks little bit different then the other one shown and can be a nice addition to your arsenal.

This one is similar to the first one but black in color and it has a ¼ inch straight end one one side and a ¼ inch angled end on the other. Any of these three styles will work.

There are also patch cables that will be used if you decide to use pedals. We will get into these in the next lesson. For now just make sure you get a good quality guitar cable to connect the guitar to the amp.

And if you decide to use pedals, be sure to get two cables.

Lesson 8: Guitar effect pedals

The reason for using guitar effect pedals is they allow for more diversity in your guitar playing. Like for instance, if your amp has two channels but no footswitch, a guitar pedal can provide this.

Let's say you like the particular tone of an overdrive or distortion pedal more than the overdrive in the amp, you can run the amp clean and use the pedal for these tones.

Or if you like reverb and don't have it in the amp, you can use a guitar pedal for this as well. With guitar pedals you can really customize your sound to be uniquely you.

What's also great about guitar pedals is that you can turn them on and off at will while playing. In fact, when you listen to your favorite songs on the radio, you will hear some of this going on. Now you know how this is done.

With guitar effect pedals.

Lesson 9: Stomp Boxes

Guitar pedals come in two forms. Stomp boxes, and effect processors. Sometimes effect processors come in the form of rack mounts, but nonetheless they are still effect processors. For this lesson, we'll focus on stomp box guitar pedals.

Stomp box guitar pedals are the most popular to use by guitar players. They are called stomp boxes because to use them, you stomp on them with your feet.

These are great accessories to have in your guitar toolbox because they come in all different sizes, shapes, colors and made by multiple manufacturing companies. This gives you the option to find the ones that are right for you.

The most popular guitar pedal that you might use will be an overdrive pedal or a distortion pedal. An overdrive pedal will give you gain or overdrive and a distortion pedal will give you more gain or distortion.

More than likely, the amp you buy will have this option in it. But since all amps are different, you might not like this effect in the amp, or you might like the sound of a particular pedal better. It doesn't matter. As long as you get the tone you desire.

Here are a few to take into consideration:

Here is an overdrive pedal made by BOSS. A very popular company when it comes to stomp boxes. With this pedal you can control the amount of level, tone & drive. Simple to set up and to use it, you just press on it with your foot for it to engage.

This is a distortion pedal made by MXR. Another very popular company when it comes to guitar pedals. As you can see, this one gives you the option to control the amount of output and distortion.

There are many to choose from in these two categories by many different companies. I recommend you do some research to find what works best for you. If you need my help, feel free email me at my website dwaynesguitarlessons.com.

In addition to overdrive/distortion pedals, you can also get creative with reverb, delay, phaser, and the infamous wah pedal.

Here is a nice reverb pedal by TC Electronics that has many options to color your guitar tone with reverb.

Reverb is an effect that sometimes comes in the amplifier itself and if that's the case, you might not need it in a pedal. But in some amps, they don't come with reverb so you might want to take a guitar pedal into consideration.

Here is a nice digital delay pedal that gives you plenty of options to color your tone. You can set the rate, effect level and delay time.

Here is another very popular pedal. The Phase 90. This has some cool sounds to it and can be fun to play with.

And of course last but not least, the wah pedal.

If you choose to use any of them, you will need additional cables. Like a daisy chain, patch cable, and a power supply. Once again these come in multiple sizes as well. But here are a few examples to get you started if you decide to go in this direction.

Daisy chain

This is needed if you are planning on powering multiple pedals at once.

Patch cable

This is needed for connecting the pedals together in the order you choose to play them in.

Power cable

This cable will power one or more guitar pedals. Most stomp boxes will also run on a 9-volt battery. So you can also use that as a power source.

Power brick

This is a power brick that you can plug all your guitar pedals into and then run one power cable to it. It provides a much nicer look and keeps things organized.

Lesson 10: Effect Processors

Guitar effect processors are another way you can go
with pedals. They are like having all the pedals shown
in the previous lesson all in one unit. This can make
them very handy.

You just have to plug one cable from your guitar into
the effects unit, and one cable from the effects unit into
the amplifier. Easy, clean and simple to use.

Here is an example of an effect processor. As you can see, it is
one single unit. It has what is called an expression pedal and
can be used as a volume and wah pedal. All the other effects I
mentioned earlier and more are in the unit.

These also come in different sizes and shapes. They can be
fun to experiment with and are loaded with musical inspiration.

Nowadays you have amplifiers that have these built into them.
These are called modeling amps. A hybrid of the amp and the
effects in one. This makes things even easier as with this
option there are no additional cables.

As you can see, when it comes to guitar effects pedals you
have plenty of options. You can get them in the amp, you can
get them in effect processor form, or you can get them as
individual stomp boxes.

Like everything else with the electric guitar, you can choose
whatever option best fits your personality and style of playing.
That is what makes playing the electric guitar so fun.

As a person just starting out, I recommend you keep it simple,
Learn the basics of the guitar first, then worry about adding
effects. It will allow you to focus on learning the guitar and less
on getting distracted.

Chapter 2 Summary

In this chapter we have learned about the amplifier and guitar effect pedals. Two very important aspects of playing electric guitar. Like I mentioned before, I recommend you keep things simple to start.

As you progress in your learning and playing, you can add more components. If you start with too much, it will just add confusion. And believe me, when it comes to learning to play the guitar, there will be plenty to focus on.

First we have the amplifier and the different types that are available. Solid state and tube or valve. Decide which one is best for you. Both have their pros and cons. So do research and get the one you prefer.

Second we have the guitar cables. These are very important as they are what bridge the gap between the guitar and the amplifier. And if you're going to use guitar pedals, you'll need additional cables for those.

Third we have the guitar pedals themselves. These are what allow you to add creativity and fun to the electric guitar when playing it. In fact, this is what makes playing electric guitar unique compared to other instruments.

<u>Fourth</u> we have the stomp box type of guitar pedals. These are individual units that usually provide one particular sound. These are great for customization of your guitar tone. Very popular and easy to use.

<u>Fifth</u> we have the effect processor and modeling amps. These are where the effects are all in one unit. These are quite nice because they eliminate all the additional cables and everything is in one place.

I recommend you study this chapter very well and get familiar with these types of amplifiers and pedals. You can start out with just guitar, cable, amplifier. Or you can choose to add an overdrive/distortion pedal to the mix.

You can even add all the other pedals I mention if you so choose. But remember, it's just going to add to your learning curve. Meaning, more things to focus on. In the next few chapters you'll have plenty to learn so keep it simple.

Chapter 3 Electric Guitar Chords

Lesson 11: Reading tablature

Before we get started actually playing the guitar, we need to learn how to read sheet music. Nothing major I assure you but some basic charts and diagrams to help us progress faster in our learning of guitar related concepts and principles.

We will be looking at how to read tablature (tabs for short) and chord charts. These will help us to build a solid foundation that we can build on later with other books of study. Remember, there is power in understanding the written word.

First we will start with reading tablature. This is a very popular modern method for learning guitar. It doesn't tell everything, but enough to get started having fun playing the instrument. After you learn to read tabs, you can try out standard notation.

Tablature is a form of sheet music consisting of 6 horizontal lines that will represent your guitar strings. With the thinnest string (first string) on the top and the thickest string (sixth string) on the bottom.

Numbers will be placed on the lines to indicate what frets you are playing on. So in basic terms, you will be working with lines and numbers. Lines that represent what string you're on and number to indicate what fret you're on.

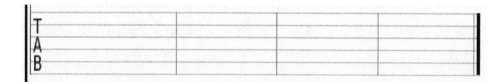

Here we have a tab diagram in four mesaures. The lines represent the 6 strings with the sixth being on the bottom.

We will then add numbers to indicate the frets that we are playing on.

Here we have a 3 on the first line. This tells us we will place our finger on the 3rd fret of the first string.

Here we have a 7 on the fourth line. This tells us that we'll place a finger on the 7th fret of the fourth string.

When playing guitar chords (which require more than one note to be played together) they will be indicated by multiple numbers on multiple lines.

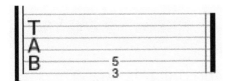

Here is an example of a power chord that is commonly played on the electric guitar. You place one finger on the 3rd fret sixth string, and place a finger on 5th fret of the fifth string.

There is more to reading tablature, and as we continue learning different techniques I'll show you more at that time. But this is the fundamental principle of how to read it. Just remember, lines, numbers and the strings are upside down.

This might be a bit confusing to read at first, but believe me it's not that difficult and it will make you a much better player in the end. Just take your time with it and let your brain absorb the information.

Now onto chord charts.

44

Lesson 12: Chord charts

Chord charts are another way to read guitar chords. These are commonly found in song books. They are square diagrams that show you where to place your fingers on each string and fret.

The only tricky part with these, is that the guitar is facing upward. Not sideways like you normally play it. That is what I like about tabs, they're written horizontal. As where chord charts are written both horizontal and vertical.

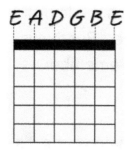

Here is an example of a guitar chord chart or diagram as it is sometimes called. The vertical lines now represent the guitar strings. With the thickest string on the left and thinnest one on the right.

The frets will be indicated by horizontal lines and not numbers like in reading tablature. The chor chart usually will represent 5 frets at a time. Six strings across from left to right and five frets down from top to bottom.

When we place a chord upon the chart it will look something like this:

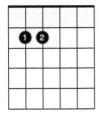

Here is an example of an E minor chord. You place a finger on the 2nd fret of the fifth string, and a finger on the 2nd fret of the fourth string.

This example also lets you know what fingers might be used to best form this chord. Sometimes this will not be available. Sometimes you just have to figure out what fingers will work best.

Same with reading tabs. They don't always indicate what fingers to use. But if you work with it enough, you'll be able to figure it out pretty easy.

As time goes on, I'll show you more examples and give you insight as to what fingers might be best to execute the chord voicings.

Lesson 13: Natural chords

In this training, we are going to be looking at three types of guitar chords. Natural chords, power chords, and barre chords. These are the most common types of chords played on the electric guitar.

Within these three categories, there are literally thousands of guitar chords that can be created. I know, crazy huh? But we don't need to learn that many. At least not right now. We just want to learn the most common ones we will run into when we start playing songs.

Natural chords are the most common. Played within the first few frets and are found in hundreds if not thousands of songs played on the guitar. These chord types will help you to form a solid chord vocabulary.

Since we are learning about reading both tablature and chord charts I will present these to you in both formats. That way you can learn to read both. The more you can read and understand about this wonderful language, the better.

E minor

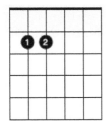

I start you off with this chord because it is the easiest to form.
Just two fingers on two strings.

E major

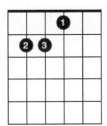

As you can see, for this chord we just add a finger on the 1st
fret third string.

These are the two easiest of all natural chords to form and that
is why I start you off here. What you will be doing, is switching
between these chords in songs. So the order you learn to form
them in can be very beneficial.

A minor

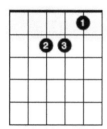

This chord shape is exactly like the E major. Except you just drop all your fingers down a string.

A major

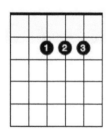

As you can see with this chord, you just move a finger over on the second string to the 3rd fret. Now all notes are on the 2nd fret to create the A major chord.

Now if we go back to our A minor formation and just move the third string up to the fifth string 3rd fret, we get the C major chord.

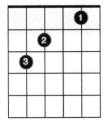

See how you can easily go from this chord to the A minor? This is very important to think about, because when learning chords, you'll need to switch between them. So you want to be aware of this.

F major

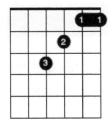

A chord that is very similar to the C major. Just move all your fingers down a string and do your best to bar the first two strings with your index finger.

50

D major

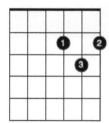

I like to think of this chord as a triangle chord. As it is in the shape of a triangle facing toward the bridge of the guitar.

D minor

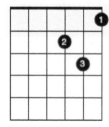

Once again, we just need to move one note to create this chord from the D major. The D and D minor are very popular. Make sure you work on forming and switching to and from them often as this will help you build finger dexterity and fluid motion.

G major

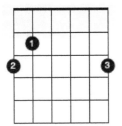

This chord I save for last as far as the main natural chords to learn. The reason for this is because of the stretch between the first and sixth strings on the 3rd fret.

You might need to take some time to get this chord down. But if you work at forming the other ones first, it will make this one a lot easier to get.

These are the most common natural chords (or open chords as they are sometimes called) that you will run into. As I stated before, there are literally thousands of chords you can learn, but we'll save that for another book.

Just focus on getting these ones down first as they will set the foundation for your guitar chord vocabulary.

Once you have that down, I recommend you learn these other common guitar chords. Some have odd names, but don't worry about that for now, just learn to play them.

52

Additional natural chords to learn

Common seventh chords

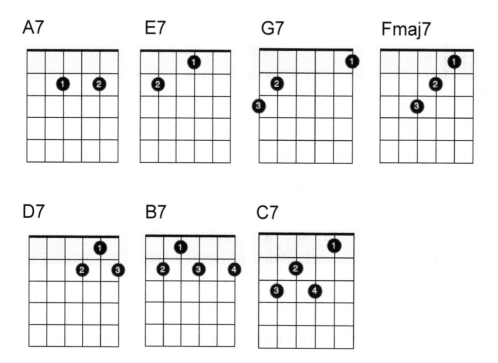

There are plenty more where these come from, but these are the most common and will get you started.

Now let's look at a few more additional chords that have weird names but are easy to play and also commonly found in songs.

Suspended and add9 chords

These chords have weird names but not to be alarmed. There
is a reason why and I will go into this a bit more in detail later in
the training. But since this is a beginner book, let's keep things
simple and just learn how to play them.

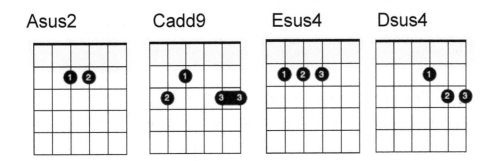

Asus2   Cadd9   Esus4   Dsus4

Fadd9

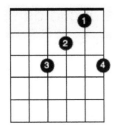

As you can see, some of these chords are similar to other ones
you've learned so far. Just on different strings or possibly
formed with different fingering. As you work with these you'll
see how they can help you to get a wide variety of sounds out
of the guitar.

Natural chords are the most common to play on both electric and acoustic guitar. Make sure you study and practice them daily. Notice how a lot of them are very similar, have only three or four notes, and all within the first few frets.

As you progress in your studies, you'll discover more that you can add to your chord vocabulary. Don't worry too much about the crazy names for now. Just learn what they are and how to form them.

If you'd like to learn more about guitar chord theory, I recommend you check out my book Rhythm Guitar Alchemy. This book teaches the science of chord construction and how to use it to improve your rhythm playing.

Now let's take a look at power chords. These types of chords will give us additional knowledge of the guitar. As these are played up and down the fretboard.

In fact, these are probably the most common in rock guitar songs. So if that's what you want to play, don't pass up this next lesson. Because once you understand these types of chords, you'll be able to play all kinds of great songs.

Lesson 14: Power chords

Power chords are almost easier to play then natural chords because they only require two fingers. You can use three to fatten up the sound, but normally you would just use two.

The only thing about these types of guitar chords, is that they require a bit of a stretch. And they move up and down the fretboard instead of staying within the first few frets like natural chords do.

Since I showed you the natural chords in chord chart form, I'll show you power chords in tablature form. As this is the most popular format you will normally see these in.

People often ask me "why are they called power chords?" Well, the reason for this is because when you add overdrive or distortion to them, they have a lot of "power" for only two or three notes.

You will see what I am saying when you start learning to play them and add the overdrive or distortion. A lot of time when learning new concepts and principles, the understanding comes when they are put into action.

This is why practical application is so important.

Like I said before, a power chord is a simple two note chord played on two strings. Mainly the three lower strings. There are exceptions that you'll run into, but for the most part they will be played on the lower strings.

The easiest power chords to form are the open power chords. There are three of these. Open E, open A, and open D. This is because of the way the notes line up on the fretboard.

The reason why these are the easiest of all guitar chords to play, is because they only require one finger. They are called open chords, because whenever you play a string without putting a finger down on it, it's considered open.

In the case of the open E, A, and D chords, one of the two strings played will be open. Here is an example of these three open chords.

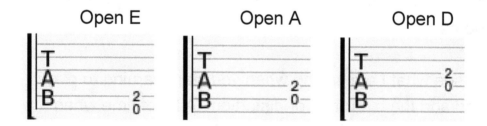

These chords have a "0" which stands for open. All you need to do is place your index finger on the second fret of the A, D, or G string to form these chords while playing both strings.

The great thing about open power chords, is that they only require one finger on the fretboard. Then you just strum the two strings that the chord is made of to play it. You don't even need to strum all six strings. Pretty easy huh?

After you learn to play those, you then learn to play the traditional power chord. With two fingers. The open power chords stay where they're at, but these move up and down the fretboard.

Here are 2 finger power chord examples:

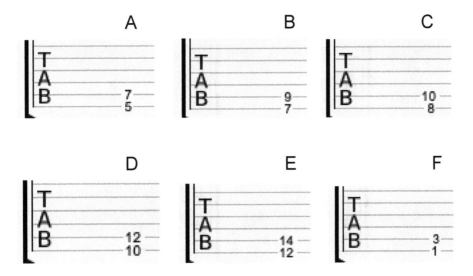

58

G

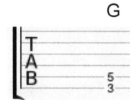

As you can clearly see, all these chords have the same shape. Unlike the natural chords we learned earlier. They also don't have names like major, minor, sus, or add9. They are much simpler than that because of the two note structure.

Here are some more examples of these types of chords. Once you get down the shape, you can play all kinds of rock songs.

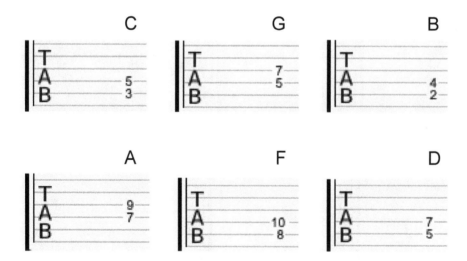

These chords can be played all over the fretboard. Same shape, just on different strings and on different frets. Be sure to practice these daily to get familiar with their locations.

Lesson 15: Barre chords

Now we come to the infamous barre chord. I say this because these chords are the hardest to form. Especially at the very beginning of your guitar playing journey. That is why I waited till now to show them to you.

What makes these chords hard to form for the beginner, is that you have to "barre" your index finger across all six strings. This acts as a moveable nut. Do you remember what the nut of the guitar is?

You also bring in your other two fingers to form this chord. This chord is like a power chord, but fuller. Think of the power chord as a simpler barre chord.

Now there are partial barre chords that you can play with one finger. I will show you those first. But it is the full barre chord that is the biggest challenge to overcome in the beginning. So I will save this chord type for last.

Partial barre chords are usually played on the two middle strings. Do you remember the names of these two strings? If not, I suggest you go back and take a look. Here are a few examples to learn.

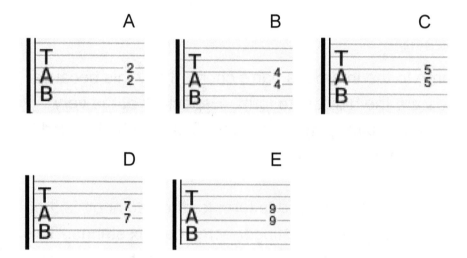

These are just some of the partial barre chords you can play.
Learn these and remember where they are located on the
fretboard. Now here are some full barre chords.

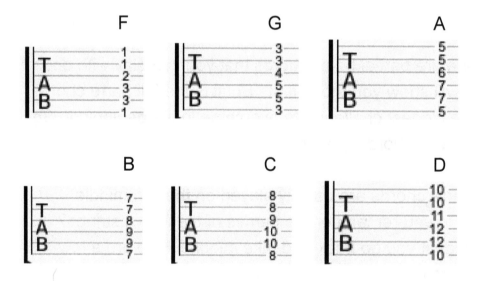

As you can see, these chords use all six strings. These ones are based off of the 6th string. These types of chords are based off of the natural E chord.

You basically use your index finger to form the nut and the rest of your fingers to form the E major chord. Then you just move them up and down the fretboard. These are considered root 6 major barre chords.

Take your middle finger off of the third string and you have a Root 6 minor barre chord. Move or add specific notes and you can create other types of guitar chords like 7ths, 9ths, sus, etc.

If we play our A minor chord and use the index finger as the nut, we can create root 5 minor barre chords.

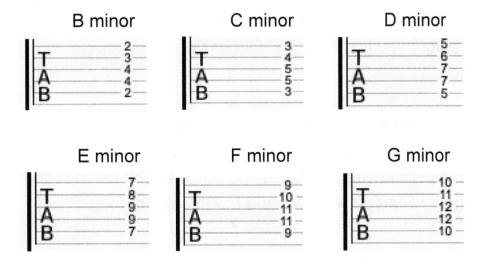

The reason I used the A minor for the root 5 barre chords is because the two chord shapes are the same. Remember that from the lesson on natural chords? The A minor chord is the same shape as the E major. Just a string down.

This allows us to use the same shape to form root 6 major barre chords and root 5 minor barre chords. To make the major and minor counterparts, you just need to move or take away certain notes within the chords.

You can use the F natural chord shape to create root 4 barre chords, but these are a bit harder to form and not quite as popular. In this case, you could just use the partial barre chords I showed you earlier.

Barre chords are not easy to play and will require some time to allow your finger muscles to develop. If you learn all the other chords I taught you first it will be a lot easier when you get to these ones.

Be sure to learn the power chord first as it will make a nice prerequisite for the full barre chord. Like I said before, you need to master the stretch. Once you do, then you can add the other fingers. Start off with two and progress from there.

Chapter 3 summary

In this chapter we have covered some very important concepts on reading sheet music and popular chord types that are played on the electric guitar.

Reading and understanding guitar chords is essential for becoming a great guitar player. The reason for this is because the guitar was originally designed as a rhythm instrument. Playing chords and creating chord progressions is how this is done.

Later in the training I will introduce you to concepts that will allow you to use it as a lead instrument. Then you will be able to pick and choose which you prefer, or be able to do both.

First we have the chord charts. A square diagram with both vertical and horizontal lines. These represent the guitar strings and the first five frets. Sometimes they will show further up the neck, and this will be indicated on the side by a fret number.

Remember, when reading these the guitar is facing upward. Not sideways like you normally play it. This will make reading and understanding chord charts easier.

Chord charts have been around forever, so i recommend you take some time to learn to read them. They will help your development tremendously. I guarantee it.

Second we have the tablature. Another form of sheet music. This is the most popular type of sheet music for guitar players. Especially in today's modern digital world.

Unlike the chord charts, we only use horizontal lines. These represent the strings and the frets will be represented by numbers. This makes it easy to understand when applied to the guitar.

You just need to remember that the strings in the sheet music will be upside down from your guitar. The reason for this is because the lowest notes are always on the bottom. This is a very important principle to understand.

Third, we learned natural chords. These are the most popular chord types to play on the electric guitar. These can also be played on the acoustic guitar. These are mainly made up into majors and minors.

Although with added, subtracted, and moved notes, a lot of other chords can be formed. Make sure you work on learning these first. They will help develop your hand and finger muscles.

Fourth, we look at power chords. These are the most popular when playing rock guitar. Songs that typically have overdrive or distortion in them. These are simple two note chords that move up and down the fretboard.

I recommend you learn these second as they will help you to develop your hands and finger muscles. The main thing with these chords is the finger stretch. Work on this and once you do, then work on moving the chords around.

Fifth, we have the infamous barre chords. These are the chords that make people want to break their guitar due to frustration. Don't do that! You can get these down if you just work at them a little at a time.

Get the power chord down first as this will really help develop two of the four fingers. Also work at getting your index finger to hold the barre. This is the hardest thing to do so work on it daily.

Once you get those two things down, you can then focus on adding the other two fingers. These types of chords will come in handy later when you learn to arpeggiate guitar chords.

Chapter 4 Creating Rhythm

Lesson 16: Strumming chords

The most common way to play the guitar chords that you have learned in the previous chapter, is to strum them. This is where you will play across all six strings with the guitar pick.

Playing guitar chords in this manner makes them sound like music. These notes are not random. They have specifically been chosen to be most enjoyable to the listener when they are played together.

You first learn to form the chords, then you learn to switch between them with your fretboard hand. While doing this, you strum them with your picking hand to create chord progressions that make up songs.

There are multiple ways you can play guitar chords. We will take a look at the most common ways. For a beginner it is strumming the chords, (playing the notes all together) and then playing the notes of the chords individually.

Strumming is a motion of moving the pick up and down across all six strings. In some cases it might be partial, but for now let's focus on strumming across all six.

68

Here are a few examples of strumming guitar chords:

Example #1 strum down

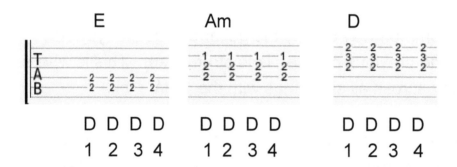

In this example we'll use three simple chords. They'll be played four times each. Each one strummed downward. This creates what is called a chord progression. Putting chords together in a select pattern. This is the basis of all songs.

Start out by forming the E minor chord. Strum across all six strings in a downward motion four times. Then switch to the next chord and do the same thing. I recommend you keep the speed slow and steady to start.

Play the chords individually slowly and listen for how the chords sound one after the other. At the end of the progression you'll go back on the E minor chord that you started on.

Example #2 strum down and up

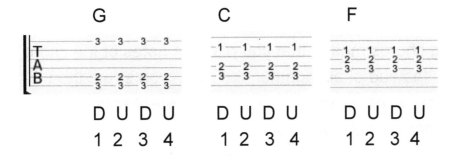

In this example you play different chords. But this time you want to strum down and back up. Down on the first and third beat, and up on the second and fourth beat. Make sure to pay close attention to this.

It will allow you to develop a better picking technique. Make sure to keep your strumming slow and steady. This works with all three chord types. When playing power chords, you only need to strum the two strings of the chord.

Lesson 17: Arpeggiating chords

Arpeggiating chords means that you play the notes of the chord individually. Instead of all together like when you strum them. This gives you an opportunity to create a different sound while developing more of your picking hand.

This is a great way to get a softer emotion out of the chords. It also allows you to hear each string more clearly and opens up a much wider opportunity for playing guitar chords.

This technique can be very beneficial to your electric guitar playing and you will notice this as you progress in your studies of learning how to get the most out of your guitar chords.

Here are some examples of this technique:

Example #1

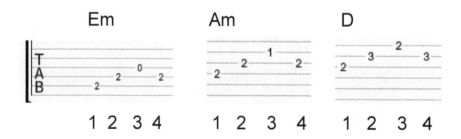

Em   Am   D

1 2 3 4   1 2 3 4   1 2 3 4

The C and G chords will require you to skip strings. This will add a nice opportunity to develop the skill of string skipping. This can add a nice touch to this picking approach.

Example #2

In these examples we arpeggiate the C chord and skip the 3rd string. For the G chord we skip the 4th, 3rd, and 2nd strings. Playing the guitar chords in this fashion will get your mind thinking a bit differently from just strumming.

Playing in this manner will inspire you to create some different sounds and allow you to get more out of your guitar chords. Try different combinations of notes within the chords. Expand on the examples that I have presented.

Use other chords you have learned so far as well. The more you work with the tools of the trade, the more you will learn how they work. You'll then get the most of them individually as well as collectively.

Lesson 18: Chord progressions

A chord progression is when you put chords together in a specific sequence. This is what provides the foundation for all songs. It is the first step to creating music.

Your fretboard hand will create the chord progression and your picking hand will create the rhythm for that chord progression. This is how both hands work together in harmony and why this motor skill development is so important.

With chord progressions you can strum the chords as well as arpeggiate them. With the knowledge and skill set of both of these two approaches, you can get a lot of diversity out of your playing. You just need to be creative.

As you do, you will hear how these techniques work in some of your favorite songs. And that my friend is when things start to get fun and interesting. A lot of songs are made up of only three or four chords.

In this lesson we will look at some very common chord progressions that are in songs. Possibly some of your favorite songs. As you get better with your study and practice, you'll begin to hear bits and pieces of them.

Here are some common chord progressions. Just keep things simple for right now. Three or four chords is all that you need at this phase in your learning. As time goes on and you get better, you can work with more complex progressions.

Chord progression #1

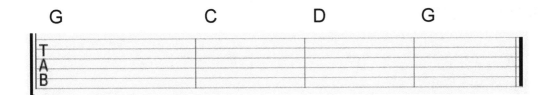

Chord progression #2

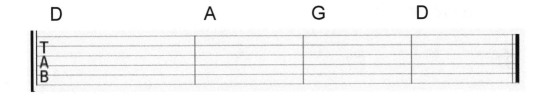

Chord progression #3

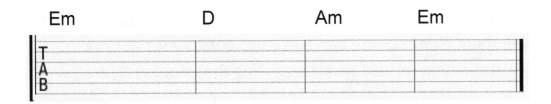

74

Chord progression # 4

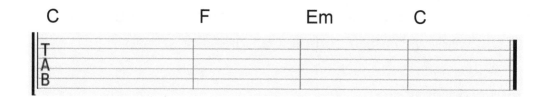

Chord progression #5

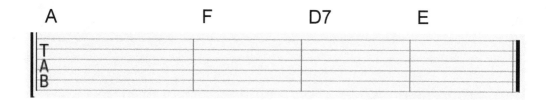

Chord progression # 6

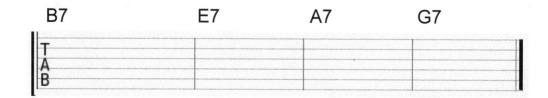

These are basic chord progressions for you to get started with.
I left them blank so you can be creative with your approach.
Try strumming as well as arpeggiating the chords.

You will begin to hear parts of songs in these progressions Use
these examples as a guide for you to create your own. Change
them around and see what you come up with.

Lesson 19: Develop good timing

One of those most important aspects of playing guitar (or any instrument for that matter) is to develop good timing. This is very important and can't be emphasised enough. Make sure not to skip this lesson.

The best way to do this is to learn about timing sequences and then practice them on a daily basis. Working with a metronome or a drum machine can help develop this skill set much quicker and is something to take into consideration.

Timing sequences can be broken down into four types of beats. Quarter notes, eighth notes, triplets, and sixteenths. In this chapter we will look at these individually and learn how to use them with the lessons we've learned so far.

<u>Quarter notes</u>

These are the most common. They are a simple 1 2 3 4 count. This means that you will count four beats per measure.

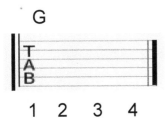

Eighth notes

This is where you add an "&" between the beats. It will now be a 1 & 2 & timing sequence. Since an 1/8th is half of a quarter, two eighth notes will equal one quarter note. Music can be broken down into simple math.

C

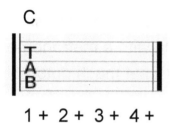

1 + 2 + 3 + 4 +

In this example, you could strum downward on the regular beats and strum up on the "&" in between. This will give you a different timing sequence then just strumming down on the quarter note beats.

Triplets

Triplets are where you play three notes tied together. This gives you a different type of feel then the quarter and eighth notes. Here you add an "uh" to the sequence. So you now have a 1 & uh, 2 & uh, etc.

D

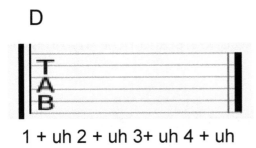

1 + uh 2 + uh 3+ uh 4 + uh

Triplets give a "galloping on a horse" feel to the rhythm and it is this feel, that makes it so unique. This can be found in many styles of music at different tempos.

<u>Sixteenth notes</u>

This is where we add an "e" to the rhythm. This gives us a different feel. Double the eighth note feel. In this rhythm sequence we have a 1 e + uh, 2 e + uh, 3 e + uh, etc.

A

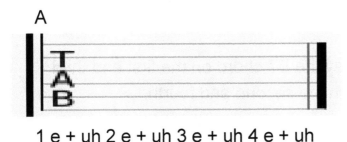

1 e + uh 2 e + uh 3 e + uh 4 e + uh

Try this rhythm slowly at first and then as you get more familiar with it you can speed it up. Do this with all the rhythms that have been presented so far.

The more you work with them you'll begin to see how they differ from each other. Once you get that down, then you can add them together. This will help you to understand how rhythms in your favorite songs are created.

We also have such things as half notes and whole notes. There are many aspects to playing rhythm guitar, but since this book is a beginners overview, I won't go into all of them here. But I'll present to you the basics to get you started.

Half notes

This is when you play a note or chord and hold it for two beats.

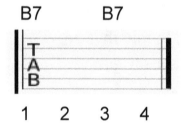

In this example, you play the B7 chord on the first and third beat, and hold it through the second and fourth.

Whole notes

This is where you play a note or chord on the first beat and hold it through the rest of the measure.

E7

1 2 3 4

Here you just play the chord on the first beat and hold it through the other three.

Like I said before, once you understand these basic concepts of creating rhythm individually, you can mix and match them.

Here is a simple example:

G G G G G G G G C   C   D   G G G G

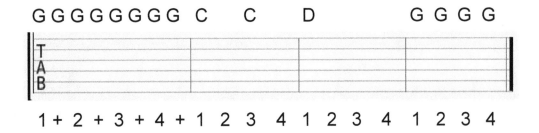

1 + 2 + 3 + 4 + 1 2 3 4 1 2 3 4 1 2 3 4

Play this and you'll hear how a certain rhythm has been created. Try this with other combinations and you'll see more clearly what I mean. This will help you develop many skills at once.

Lesson 20: Guitar riffs

One of the funnest things to do when playing guitar is to play guitar riffs. You can do this with all chord types. Natural chords, power chords, and barre chords.

A guitar riff is a recognizable sample of music. Something you play and people say "that sounds familiar"" and it is this guitar riff that makes you feel good about your playing.

Here are a few ways you can put chords together to play guitar riffs.

Example #1

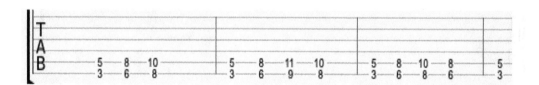

Example #2

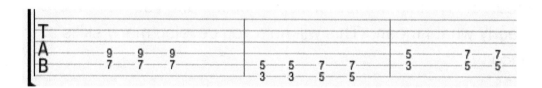

Example #3

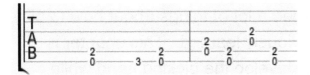

Example #4

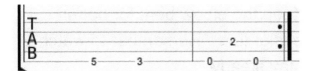

Example #5

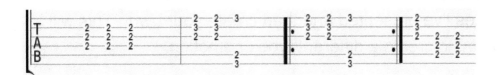

Example #6

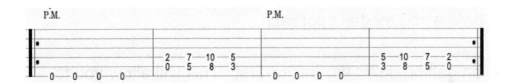

In this last example the PM stands for palm muting. This is where you rest the palm of your picking hand on the string to create a percussive sound. Very popular in guitar playing.

Chapter 4 Summary

In this chapter we have learned a lot of things about how to play the chords that we have previously learned. This chapter is very important as it helps to develop the picking hand while creating rhythm.

First, there is strumming the chords. Here we want to make sure to keep a loose wrist. Keep the elbow bent for better positioning and relax for an easier flow. Remember to watch your tempo, as you want to stay steady.

Second, there is arpeggiating the chords. This is where the notes of the chords are played individually. Start with the examples I've presented and then create your own. This will allow you to create a different type of emotion.

These are the two most common ways to approach playing guitar chords. Make sure to master these first. You can also play with your fingers, but I recommend you learn to work with a pick before you try this approach.

Focus on getting down the basics first. This will allow you to build a solid foundation for all other learning to stand on. It will make it easier to progress in the future.

Third, we have chord progressions. This is where we take the chords that have been learned, and put them into a particular sequence. A certain pattern. This is what all songs no matter the style are made of.

Make sure you fully understand this part of the chapter, because it will lay the groundwork. This will give you a better understanding of song construction for learning and writing your own.

Fourth, we have timing. Develop good timing. I can't stress the importance of this enough. I have met many musicians over the years that have not developed this skill. Like they missed the lesson all together.

Do not do this. Learn and fully understand about the notes of timing that I have presented. Quarter, eighth, triplet, sixteenth, half, & whole notes. There are more, but for now, focus your attention on these.

Fifth, we have guitar riffs.

This is where guitar playing really gets fun. Playing guitar riffs. As you progress with your studies and master concepts and techniques, bits and pieces of familiarity will start to develop to your ear.

Take note of this. As you will see, they all use these concepts and techniques that you are learning in this book. Once this begins to happen, a sense of accomplishment is built. You begin to venture out of your comfort zone.

You begin to see what else is out there to learn. But in order to develop this, you must master the fundamentals. The chords, how to play them, put them together, and how to create a solid rhythm.

Do all this and you will become a great rhythm guitar player. You will also be ready for what comes next. How to play lead guitar. This requires a bit more practice, but well worth the time invested.

So if you're ready, let's venture on.

Chapter 5 Playing Lead Guitar

Lesson 21: Major scale

Now that we have learned how to play rhythm guitar, we can progress into what is known as lead guitar. This is where we will focus on creating melody with single notes.

Harmony is when we play notes together as in chords, and melody is when we play single notes as in scales. These are what we will discuss in this chapter. What scales are and how to use them to play lead guitar.

Like chords, there are thousands of scales that can be played on the guitar. As with the chords, we don't need to learn that many. Just the main ones that are most common. That is what we will learn in this chapter.

The first scale we want to learn is the major scale. This is the Do Re Mi that we learn as a child in school. If you didn't learn this then, no worries because you're going to learn it now.

The major scale is, Do Re Mi Fa So La Ti Do. A selection of 8 notes (actually 7 as the 8th note duplicates the first to double its frequency) that make up a certain key. The most common way to categorize western music.

To make things simple we will learn the notes of the C major scale. The reason for this is because this scale does not have any sharps or flats in it.

C major: C D E F G A B C

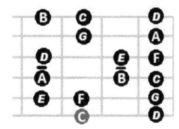

This is what's called a scale box pattern. The reason for this is because of the way the notes line up. Learn this scale and get familiar with it. It will come in very handy when it comes to playing a guitar solo in the key of C major.

Remember, scales are notes played individually. So in this case you want to start with the C note on the 8th fret and progress through the scale. The D note, E, F, and so forth. This is how melody is created.

Once you learn the note patterns, you can then learn how to use them to create musical melodies and cool guitar solos with techniques associated with lead guitar playing. But first, let's learn the note patterns.

Here are a few more in different keys written in tab format.

G major scale: G A B C D E F# G

```
-2----3----------5--
------3----------5--
-2---------4-----5--
-2---------4-----5--
-2----3----------5--
------3----------5--
```

This is the same thing as above, you just play it at the third fret because that is where the G note is located. Also notice that this G note is where you play the G major chord.

D major scale: D E F# G A B C# D

```
-9----10----------12-
------10----------12-
-9----------11-----12-
-9----------11-----12-
-9----10----------12-
------10----------12-
```

As you can see, these three scales all have the same pattern. The notes just change because of the location along the fretboard. This makes them very easy to play within a certain key.

They also have an added note at the end because the scale would just start over again. Once you learn the notes of the fretboard (in a later lesson) you'll see how this works.

This will allow you to travel all over the fretboard and stay in key every time. The most common issue with guitar solos among guitar players, is staying in key. This will help to solve this issue.

Here are a couple more,

A major scale: A B C# D E F# G# A

```
--4------5----------7--
---------5----------7--
--4-----------6-----7--
--4-----------6-----7--
--4------5----------7--
---------5----------7--
```

E major scale: E F# G# A B C# D# E

```
-11---12------------14-
------12------------14-
-11-----------13----14-
-11-----------13----14-
-11---12------------14-
------12------------14-
```

These are very common major scales to play on guitar. Make sure you master their pattern of notes and location.

Lesson 22: Natural minor scale

Like the minor chord, we also have a minor scale. Actually there are several different ones, but the most common will be the natural minor scale. This is what we will focus on here in this lesson.

Remember, scales are very much like chords. A selection of notes played in a specific order. The only difference is that you normally play notes of a chord together, and notes of a scale you play individually.

When you take the 3rd, 6th, and 7th notes of the major scale and flatten them by one fret, you get what is called a natural minor scale.

Example:

C Major scale: C D E F G A B C

C minor scale: C D Eb F G Ab Bb C

As you can see, the E, A, and B have been flattened by one fret and are now E flat, A flat, and B flat. This is how all natural minor scales will be created. Remember this, and you will be able to create this scale very easily every time.

Here are some examples of the natural minor scale.

C minor scale: C D Eb F G Ab Bb C

```
|-------8--------------10----11--|
|-------8------9------------11---|
|-7-----8--------------10-------|
|-------8--------------10--------|
|-------8--------------10----11--|
|-------8--------------10----11--|
```

As you can see, this scale presents a different pattern of notes now that we have flattened a few. It is this change up in pattern that gives the scale its character. Listen to how it sounds compared to its major counterpart.

G minor scale: G A Bb C D Eb F G

```
|-------3------------5----6---|
|-------3------4----------6---|
|-2-----3------------5-------|
|-------3------------5-------|
|-------3------------5----6---|
|-------3------------5----6---|
```

In this major scale the F note that is sharp, now becomes a natural F because we flattened it. Any sharp note in the 3rd, 6th, or 7th position in the major scale, will become a natural note when flattened.

This is very important to recognize and understand when creating scales of different kinds. It is this movement of certain notes that give the scales their color and character.

D minor scale: D E F G A Bb C D

```
------10-------12-13-
------10--11------13-
-9--10-------12------
----10-------12------
----10-------12-13-
----10-------12-13-
```

In this scale we have one flat note. The B flat. The F and C notes that were sharpened are now natural. Notice also that the box pattern is the same as in the other scales.

A minor scale: A B C D E F G A

```
------5-------7--8--
------5--6-------8--
-4--5-------7------
----5-------7------
----5-------7--8--
----5-------7--8--
```

In this minor scale, since all three sharp notes are in the 3rd, 6th, and 7th position, they all become natural. This means that this scale is relative to the C major because they both consist of the same notes.

Just like the major scale. Practice this scale and get familiar with it in different locations on the fretboard. It will help you to solo over minor key chord progressions.

Lesson 23: Minor pentatonic scale

Now we come to the most common scale for playing guitar solos and melody lines. The minor pentatonic scale. The reason for this is because it works well with a lot of different styles of music.

It is also a scale of only five notes. Penta meaning five and tonic meaning notes. A five note scale. Pretty easy to deal with right? Five notes with endless possibilities.

If you master only one scale, (which I hope for your guitar playing you master them all) I recommend it be this one. This is usually the one that everyone who plays guitar solos starts out with.

Once again, like the other two scales we just learned, it is presented in a simple box pattern for easier understanding and playing. Almost all great guitar players in all styles of music have used this scale at one time or another.

This scale can be found in Blues, Pop, Country, Jazz, and of course Rock music. The reason for this is because of the note intervals and how they seem to just fit so many things in music of all types.

The minor pentatonic scale comes out of the minor scale. We simply pick five notes and only play them. These five notes will be the 1, b3, 4, 5, and b7. These will be the notes in any key you choose to create them out of.

A major scale: A B C# D E F# G# A

A minor scale: A B C D E F G A

A minor pentatonic scale: A C D E G

See how we use the 1, b3, 4, 5, and b7 that are taken out of the minor scale? This can be done with all minor scales in the music spectrum.

A minor pentatonic scale: A C D E G

```
—5———————————8—
—5———————————8—
—5————————7————
—5————————7————
—5————————7————
—5———————————8—
```

See how simple this scale pattern is? Very easy to read and very easy to understand. And just like the other scale patterns we've learned, the pattern will be the same for all keys. It is just the notes on the fretboard location that will change.

G minor pentatonic scale: G Bb C E F

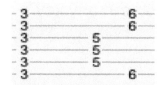

Here the F that is normally F# becomes a natural F and the natural B now becomes a B flat.

C minor pentatonic scale: C Eb F G Bb

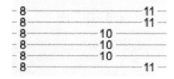

Here we have two flats in the scale because these two notes are normally natural.

D minor pentatonic scale: D F G A C

```
-10 ------------- 13 --
-10 ------------- 13 --
-10 ------- 12 ------
-10 ------- 12 ------
-10 ------- 12 ------
-10 ------------- 13 --
```

In this scale no flats are presented because the F & C are
normally sharp.

E minor pentatonic scale: E G A B D

```
-12 ------------- 15 --        0 ------------- 3 --
-12 ------------- 15 --        0 ------------- 3 --
-12 ------- 14 ------          0 ------- 2 ------
-12 ------- 14 ------          0 ------- 2 ------
-12 ------- 14 ------          0 ------- 2 ------
-12 ------------- 15 --        0 ------------- 3 --
```

This scale also has no flats, and is presented in two positions.
The closed position (like the others) at the 12th fret (where the
E note is located) and in the open position.

Since the guitar is in the pitch of E (in normal standard tuning)
we can play this scale close to the nut in what's called an open
position. This is because of the open notes being used. Same
notes, just in a different location on the fretboard.

Notice the notes change, but the pattern stays the same.

Lesson 24: Major pentatonic scale

In addition to the minor pentatonic scale, we also have a major pentatonic scale. So we will look at this next. This is a great scale as well and can be played over major and minor keys if played in the correct location.

In this scale, we will use the 1, 2, 3, 5, and 6th notes of the major scale. No flats. In fact, an easy way to remember this scale is that it is a major scale minus the 4th and 7th notes.

Since this is the case, the pattern of notes will be presented a bit differently. This pattern for all keys will stay the same, just the notes will change. This is what's fantastic about these scales.

The way the notes line up on the fretboard, you just need to move them around. Very much like the power and barre chords we learned in the rhythm section. The form stays the same and the notes change automatically to fit what we need.

How cool is that?

Very cool if you ask me.

G major pentatonic scale: G A B D E

```
--------------3------------5---
--------------3------------5---
-2-------------------4---------
-2-------------------------5---
-2-------------------------5---
--------------3------------5---
```

A major pentatonic scale: A B C# E F#

```
--------------5------------7---
--------------5------------7---
-4-------------------6---------
-4-------------------------7---
-4-------------------------7---
--------------5------------7---
```

C major pentatonic scale: C D E G A

```
--------------8-----------10---
--------------8-----------10---
-7-------------------9---------
-7------------------------10---
-7------------------------10---
--------------8-----------10---
```

D major pentatonic scale: D E F# A B

```
-------------10-----------12---
-------------10-----------12---
-9------------------11---------
-9------------------------12---
-9------------------------12---
-------------10-----------12---
```

Make sure to master this scale as well.

Lesson 25: Blues scale

Now we come to the infamous blues scale. A six note scale that has the flat three or flat five in it. This depends on if you're playing major or minor blues. These are the two scales we'll look at in this lesson.

What is great about this scale, is that it is easy to learn and even easier to use because it is the same pattern as the major and minor pentatonic scales, with just an added note. For the major you add the b3rd, and for the minor, the b5th.

Remember how the pentatonic scale is based on five notes? Well just add one more in a certain location, and you have the blues scale. Pretty cool huh?

This scale is very popular in a lot of music because of this note that is added. It gives a very dark moody sound to the music. So if you ever want to play or create melodies of this type, look no further than the blues scale.

A major scale: A B C# D E F# G# A
A major pentatonic scale: A B C# E F#
A major blues scale: A B C C# E F# (added flat 3rd)
A minor pentatonic scale: A C# D E G
A minor blues scale: A C# D Eb E G (added flat 5th)

A major blues scale: A B C C# E F#

```
-----5-------7--8--
-----5-------7-----
-4---5---6---------
-4-----------7-----
-4-----------7-----
-----5-------7--8--
```

G major blues scale: G A Bb B D E

```
-----3-------5--6--
-----3-------5-----
-2---3---4---------
-2-----------5-----
-2-----------5-----
-----3-------5--6--
```

C major blues scale: C D Eb E G A

```
-----8------10--11-
-----8------10-----
-7---8---9---------
-7----------10-----
-7----------10-----
-----8------10--11-
```

D major blues scale: D E F F# A B

```
----10------12--13-
----10------12-----
-9--10--11---------
-9----------12-----
-9----------12-----
----10------12--13-
```

A minor blues scale: A C D Eb E G

```
-5-------------8-
-5-------------8-
-5--------7----8-
-5--------7------
-5---6----7------
-5-------------8-
```

G minor blues scale: G Bb C Db D F

```
-3-------------6-
-3-------------6-
-3--------5----6-
-3--------5------
-3---4----5------
-3-------------6-
```

E minor blues scale: E G A Bb B D

```
-12-----------15-        -0------------3-
-12-----------15-        -0------------3-
-12------14---15-        -0-------2----3-
-12------14------        -0-------2------
-12--13--14------        -0---1---2------
-12-----------15-        -0------------3-
```

C minor blues scale: C Eb F Gb G Bb

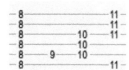

```
-8------------11-
-8------------11-
-8-------10---11-
-8-------10------
-8---9---10------
-8------------11-
```

Notice where the note location is for both the major and minor.

Chapter 5 Summary

In this chapter we have learned the five most common scale types for playing lead guitar. Like I said before, there are many scales that can be played, but these are the most common and I recommend you start here first.

These will allow you to build a solid foundation of scale patterns and fretboard knowledge. Lead guitar playing is about scales as rhythm playing is about chords. Sometimes you can mix the two but you must first fully understand how they work.

First, there is the major scale. This the tree trunk that all other scales branch out from. So you want to make sure you understand it very well. This goes for chords also.

This scale is presented across the fretboard in two octaves in multiple positions. Get familiar with the Do Re Mi sound when you play it. This will help to train your ear.

Second, there is the natural minor scale. I say natural because there are other minor scales. What we want to focus on here for right now is the natural minor.

To create this scale out of any major scale, we want to flatten the 3rd, 6th, and 7th notes. Very important to remember when creating this scale.

<u>Third</u>, there is the minor pentatonic scale. This is the most common scale to play guitar solos because it works so well. The notes line up in such a way that you just can't go wrong with it.

This scale is made up of five notes taken out of the minor scale. With a flat 3rd and flat 7th note in it. Learn this scale pattern very well and listen to how the notes sound over chord progressions in the same key.

<u>Fourth</u>, there is the major pentatonic scale. This scale works great as well, except this one uses different notes. Since it is major, we don't flatten the 3rd note. We keep it natural.

By keeping the note natural, it gives it a different tone color than the minor pentatonic. This scale is made up of the 1, 2, 3, 5, and 6th notes of the major scale.

<u>Fifth</u>, we have the blues scale. Both major and minor. This scale is easy too because it can be played in both pentatonic scales. You just add a note.

You add the flat 3rd for the major blues scale, and the flat 5th for the minor blues scale. This will give the scale a more dark and moody sound.

Now, let's learn how to turn these scales into music.

Chapter 6 Lead Guitar Techniques

Lesson 26: Hammer-ons & pull-offs

Now that we know a few scales, we want to learn how to use them to play guitar solos and melody lines. This is the essence of playing lead guitar. Knowing the notes is not enough, we must learn how to express them.

This chapter is going to introduce you to the most common ways to play the notes in the scales that you have learned so far. These will also work with any other scale you choose to learn in the future.

The first techniques we'll learn are the hammer-on and pull-off. This is where we play a note and hammer-on to another without picking it, or we play a note and pull-off to another one without picking it.

These two techniques are the most common in lead guitar playing. So we will focus on them first. Think of hammer-ons and pull-offs like adding and subtracting in math. A hammer-on adds a note, and a pull-off takes a note away.

104

Here are some examples:

Hammer-on

Here we pick the 5th fret on the 3rd string and hammer-on the 7th fret with our third finger.

Pull-off

Here we have a finger on the 5th and 7th frets and we pick the 7th fret. Then pull-off to the 5th.

Hammer-on pull-off

Here we hammer-on to the 7th fret and pull-off back to the 5th all in one motion.

This same thing can be done in reverse with a pull-off hammer on.

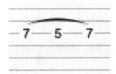

Here we pull-off from the 7th fret to the 5th and then we hammer-on back to the 7th fret.

Here are some more examples within the scales:

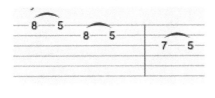

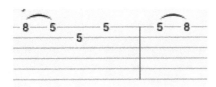

Work with these concepts and try them out with all the scales that you have learned on a daily basis.

Lesson 27: Bends & slides

The next technique we want to learn is how to bend and slide the notes. Great techniques that add a lot of expression to the creative process. You can do different types of bends, and you can slide notes up and down the fretboard.

Here are some examples of these two techniques:

Bends

Here we have bends at the 7th fret on the third string. Even though the bend is going toward the first string, you usually will bend up and not down. I know it seems backwards, but it's just the way it's written. So don't get confused by it.

Bend release

Here we have a bend up and release back down at the 9th fret of the third string and proceed to pick the 7th and 5th frets.

Work with this simple technique with other notes in the scales. Bend strings up, down and work on the bend release. You will find these techniques to be very common in guitar solos.

Slides

Here is where we play a note and slide from one to the other. We can slide up or down from any fret we choose. For now just stick with the frets that are in the scales. That way you'll learn to stay in key.

Slide up

Here we pick the 5th fret on the third string and slide up to the 7th fret on the third string.

Slide down

-7 ﹨ 5-

Here we do the opposite. Pick the 7th fret on the third string and slide down to the 5th fret on the third string.

108

Slide up and down

Here we slide up to the 9th fret and the back down to the 7th fret on the third string.

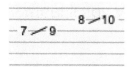

Here we have two slide ups on the 7th and 8th frets on the third and second strings.

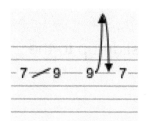

Here is an example of the slide and bend technique used together. Slide up to the 9th fret, bend and release it, then pick the 7th fret. All on the third string.

These are just some examples of how these two techniques work. Try them out with other notes and listen for how they give the notes character when applied properly.

Lesson 28: Vibrato & trills

Now we come to vibrato and trills. Vibrato is where you vibrate the note. Very much like a singer does with their vocal cords. A trill is a quick repeated hammer-on pull-off. Two very cool techniques that add expression to the notes.

Vibrato

Here we pick the 5th fret on the third string and vibrate the note up and down to give a vibrato effect.

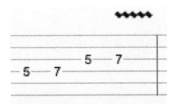

This is the same thing with a few more notes. The vibrato is now on the 7th fret of the third string.

```
~~~~    ~~~~         ~~~~    ~~~~
--3------5----------7------9--------
------------------|----------------
------------------|----------------
------------------|----------------
------------------|----------------
```

These are all on one string. One played after the other. Try doing this with different notes. Listen for how they sound.

Trills

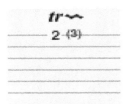

Here we pick the 2nd fret and repeatedly hammer-on to the 3rd fret on the first string.

```
tr~          tr~              tr~          tr~
                                7 (9)       10(12)
              5 (6)
--3 (4)-------------------|------------------
-------------------------|------------------
-------------------------|------------------
```

Here we have the same thing, just over multiple strings. Notice how the 7th and 10th frets trill to the 9th and 12th frets.

Work on these two techniques individually, then try to put them together and see what kind of cool sounds you come up with. You just might amaze yourself.

Lesson 29: Harmonics

Harmonics are a very cool technique that are associated with playing guitar. We have artificial harmonics and we have pinched harmonics. Artificial give you a "bell" type of sound and the pinched give more of a "squeal" type of sound.

Artificial harmonics work, when you slightly touch the guitar string over a certain fret wire and you produce a "bell chime" type of sound. It's so unique that when you get it you know it.

```
       A.H.
------------7------------
-------------------------
-------------------------
-------------------------
-------------------------
-------------------------
```

You pick the first string open, and slightly touch the note above the 7th fretwire. Not the 7th fret, but the fret wire. This will produce a bell chime effect.

```
   A.H.   A.H.   A.H.   A.H.
----7-------------------------
----------7-------------------
----------------7-------------
----------------------7-------
------------------------------
------------------------------
```

Here we slightly touch the fretwire like before, but on all four guitar strings. One right after another. This may take a little time to get, but well worth the effort.

112

Pinch harmonics

These are done with the picking hand, and will take some time
to master. But once again, well worth the time invested.

With these types of harmonics, you need to slightly rub your
thumb over the guitar string after you pick it. The artificial
harmonics are created with the fretboard hand, as where these
are created with your picking hand.

These produce more of a "squeal" type of sound. So the next
time you hear something like that in one of your favorite songs,
that's more than likely what it is.

```
P.H.            P.H.
------------------------------------
------------------------------------
--5----7----5----7------------------
------------------------------------
------------------------------------
------------------------------------
```

As you can see, these are read the same way except you have
a P.H instead of an A.H to indicate what type of harmonic it is.

These work really well when you have overdrive or distortion on
the guitar. It helps them to ring out better.

If you don't get them right away, don't get frustrated. Just keep
at it. It took me a while to get them myself.

Lesson 30: Phrasing

Here is where we take all these techniques that we have learned and combine them together, This will create what is called phrasing. Where we get the scale notes to sound like music.

Here we have a hammer-on pull-off on the 3rd fret of the first string and a vibrato on the 5th fret of the second string.

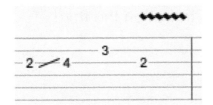

Here we have a slide from the 2nd fret to the 4th fret on the third string. Followed by a note on the 3rd fret of the second string and a 2nd fret vibrato back on the third string.

114

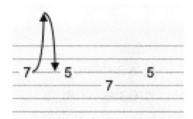

Here we have a bend release at the 7th fret third string followed by notes at the 7th and 5th frets on the fourth and third strings.

Here we have bends at the 8th and 7th frets of the first, and second strings followed by a note at the 5th fret of the second string ending with a bend release at the 7th fret on the third string.

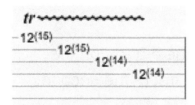

Here we have trills all at the 12th fret. On the first two strings we trill to the 15th fret and to the 14th fret on the third and fourth strings.

This is how you create phrasing with lead guitar techniques.

Chapter 6 Summary

In this chapter we have touched on the basics of playing lead guitar. There is plenty more where this comes from, just like the chords. The best thing to do is master the fundamental concepts and then proceed from there.

First, we have the hammer-ons and pull-offs. These are like adding and subtracting in math. We pick a note and hammer on to another one without picking the second note.

With a pull-off, we hold down two notes, pick the highest pitched note and pull-off back to the lowest pitched note without picking it.

Second, we have bends and slides. With bends we pick a note and bend it up. Or we can bend it up and release it for a bend release. Work on mastering both of these types of bends.

Slides are a great way to express notes and can be done either up the fretboard or down the fretboard. Practice sliding both ways.

These few techniques alone can give you some great note expression of the scales that you have learned in the previous chapter. But we have more.

<u>Third</u>, we have vibrato & trills. These are very cool techniques also. Vibrato gives a chance to express our notes very much like a vocalist vibrates their vocal cords.

Trills are a cool way to practice finger strength by repeatedly hammering on to a note. Practice the examples presented and then create your own.

<u>Fourth</u>, we have harmonics. These create really neat sounds too. The artificial harmonics aren't too hard to master. Just make sure you do them above the fretwire. They work best at certain frets.

The pinch harmonics will take some time to master but can be done and create an awesome sound on the guitar. You just need to master rubbing your thumb across the string after you pick it.

<u>Fifth</u>, we have phrasing. This is where we put all these techniques together to create music. Listen to your favorite songs when they come to the guitar solo. You'll hear how the lead guitar player uses phrasing to sound awesome.

Know that you can do this too. You just need to study and practice as they have done. This book will help you to get started and head in the right direction.

Chapter 7 Basic Music Theory

Lesson 31: Notes on the fretboard

When it comes to music theory, the best place to start is with the notes on the guitar fretboard. This is where all the mystery lies and needs to be unlocked. All the chords and scales are derived from these notes.

Regardless of whether a guitar player studies the notes, or chooses not too and just plays by ear, these notes along the fretboard are the key to master.

Now before we get to that, we want to start with the musical alphabet. These are the 12 notes that all western music is made up of.

Musical alphabet: A A# B C C# D D# E F F# G G#

This can also be called the chromatic scale. All the chords and scales that we've learned so far, come out of these twelve notes. In fact, any chords and scales that you learn in the future will come out of these as well.

118

So make sure you master these twelve notes. Also take note that each note has a sharp after it except two. Can you tell which two they are? They are the B & E. Be sure to remember this when studying your notes.

Notes along the fretboard:

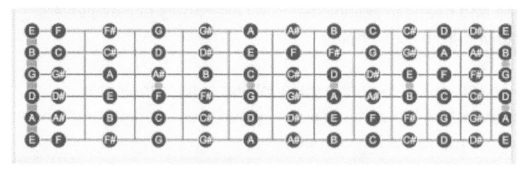

Here we have all the notes on the guitar fretboard. From a distance it can look very confusing, but if you break it down into individual strings it's not so bad.

If you take the first string (your high e string) you'll see the notes start with E and go through the musical alphabet that we learned earlier. Play the string open and that is an E note. The same name as the string itself.

If you do the same with the other 5 strings, you'll see that the notes open are B, G, D, A, and E. Then all you need to do is proceed through the music alphabet on each fret. Just start with that particular note.

Lesson 32: How chords are created

Now that we know the notes in the musical alphabet that all chords come out of, let's take a look at how the chords we've previously learned were created to begin with. This will help you understand why they are called major, minor, 7th, etc.

Major chord:

A major chord is made up of three notes taken out of the scale of 8 notes it is created from. Remember the Do Re Mi we learned earlier? That is the major scale or key.

Let's look at C major. C D E F G A B C
                              1 2 3 4 5 6 7 8

To make a C major chord we use the 1 3 5 of this scale. To make C minor we use the same three notes, but we flatten the 3rd.

So in the above example to create a C major we would use the notes C, E, and G. To make a C minor we would use the same notes except we would flatten the E to E flat. We would then use the notes C, Eb, and G to create the minor.

This philosophy works with all major and minor chords in all 12 keys in the music alphabet. Since we have 12 notes, we can create 12 keys.

7th chords

To create a 7th chord or add 9 chords, we just add more notes to the triad. The 1 3 5 is called a triad because these chords are made up of three notes. This is the foundation of all guitar chords.

A CM7 chord would just be adding the natural 7th note to the triad. We learned that the C major triad is C, E, and G, now we just need to add the B note to create the CM7 chord.

To make the C7 chord, we do the same thing except we flatten the 7th note before we add it to the C major triad. Do this and we now have this chord.

Add9 chords

With these chords we would need to go into the second octave of the scale. The reason for this is because the 9th is the same as the 2nd note in the first octave. So in the key of C, the 2nd is a D. This is the note we add to create this chord.

C add9 would be C E G D.

Lesson 33: How scales are created

Scales are created very much the same. We just take certain notes out of the key they are created from to form the scale. No matter if the scale is major or minor. The only difference is you won't have 7th and add9 like you do with chords.

Major scale

This will be all 8 notes taken out of the musical alphabet. All major scales must have the Do Re Mi sound to it. In fact if it doesn't, it's not the major scale.

Natural minor scale

Here we have the same thing except we flatten a few notes to make this scale. Do you remember what notes are flattened? They are the 3rd, 6th, and 7th notes. Do this with any major scale and you'll create the natural minor everytime.

Minor pentatonic scale

In this scale we just use five of the notes taken out of the scale. We can take these out of the natural minor scale.

C natural minor: C D Eb F G Ab Bb C
C minor pentatonic: C Eb F G Bb

Major pentatonic scale

Here we do the same thing. We just do it with the major key and use different notes than the minor. With this scale we use all notes except the 4 and 7 of the key.

C major scale: C D E F G A B C
C major pentatonic: C D E G A

If you can remember that, you'll be able to create this scale out of any key you choose. Just eliminate the 4 and 7 and you'll have the major pentatonic scale.

Blues scale

Here we do the same thing, except we add the flat 3rd or flat 5th to the pentatonic scales.

C major pentatonic: C D E G A
C major blues scale: C D Eb E G A

C minor pentatonic scale: C Eb F G Bb
C minor blues scale: C Eb F Gb G Bb

Study this lesson and go through the notes in your scales and you'll see this all to be true. This is how scales are created within the musical alphabet.

Lesson 34: Octaves & intervals

Octaves and intervals are important to know because they give more understanding to the chords and scales that we've just learned to create.

Octaves

An octave is where you have two notes that are the same but just a pitch apart. If you study your fretboard diagram you'll notice how notes are the same on each string, but just in a different location.

Like for instance, the note on the D string is the same as the note on the low E string except two frets up. This goes for the G and A string as well. This is great insight because it allows you to find notes on different strings very quickly.

```
|--------------------------|--------------------|------------11---------13--|
|--------------------------|------7---------9---|------------------------|
|------3---------5---------|--------------------|------8---------10------|
|--------------------------|----5---------7-----|------------------------|
|--1---------3-------------|--------------------|------------------------|
```

Here we have examples of octaves. Notes that are the same but on different strings and in different locations. Try these out and through your study of the guitar fretboard, see if you can find others.

124

Intervals

An interval is the distance between two or more notes. This is important to know because it relates to note location. Like we just learned with the octaves. As you study the fretboard you'll begin to make the connection.

Intervals tell us what notes need to be played to create certain chords and scales. Like the ones that we learned in previous lessons. This can be broken down into half steps and whole steps.

A half step is the distance of one fret. Like in the musical alphabet, the B and C, and the E and F notes are right next to each other with no sharp in between. These notes would be considered a half step apart.

A A# B C C# D D# E F F# G G#

A whole step is the distance of two frets. Like in the example above, the D and E would be a whole step apart because they have a note in between them. The D#. This tells us that notes like the A to B, C to D, and F to G, are all a whole step apart.

Three frets apart like from the A to the C would be considered a step and a half. A whole step between the A and B, and a half step between the B and C.

Lesson 35: Chord & scale formulas

Music is not only a language, but a science of mathematics.
The reason for this is because we deal with numbers (math)
and we deal with formulas (science) and it is this combination
that allows us to understand how this all works.

Chord formulas

We touched on this a bit earlier, but we;ll go over it again here
in a bit more detail. When we look at guitar chords from a
music theory perspective, we can clearly see there is a certain
formula to the construction of them.

The major triad chord is a 1 3 5 formula. Every major chord will
be made up of this.

The minor triad chord is the same thing except we flatten the
3rd note. So it becomes a formula of 1 b3 5. Every minor
chord will be made up of this.

Augmented triad will consist of the formula 1 3 #5 in any key.

Diminished triad will consist of the formula 1 b3 b5 in any key.

Dominant 7 (like a C7) will have the 1 3 5 b7 formula.

126

Scale formulas

Like I mentioned before, scale formulas are very similar and always the same. This is what I mean about the science of mathematics. 1+1 will always equal 2 every time. That's the science part.

A major triad in any key will always consist of the 1 3 5 of the key it is created out of. Same with scales. Certain notes of the music alphabet will be used to create the scales as well.

Major scale: 1 2 3 4 5 6 7 8

Natural minor scale: 1 2 b3 4 5 b6 b7 8

Minor pentatonic scale: 1 b3 4 5 b7

Major pentatonic scale: 1 2 3 5 6

Major blues scale: 1 2 b3 3 5 6

Minor blues scale: 1 b3 4 b5 5 b7

Remember, these scale formulas are the same no matter what key you choose to play them in. You just need to figure out what notes are in the key that relate to these numbers. Do this and you will be able to create these scales at will.

Chapter 7 Summary

In this chapter we have covered some basics of music theory as it relates to what we've learned so far. Notes, chords, and scales.

First, we start with the notes on the fretboard. This is the most important thing to know as far as music theory is concerned. All chords and scales come out of these notes.

Remember, there are 12 notes in the music alphabet and all have a sharp after them except for B, and E. So if you're on an A note, the next will be A#. But if you're on an E note, the next note will be F.

Second, we have the knowledge of how to create guitar chords. This comes from knowing the notes on the fretboard. Knowing that certain notes are used to create them.

Majors, minors, 7ths, add 9's, etc. All these and more chords are created with the 12 notes of the music alphabet. Just like words created out of our regular alphabet.

Third, there is the knowledge of creating scales. Like chords, there are literally thousands that can be made on the guitar. But for now just focus on the ones you've learned so far.

Remember what notes are needed for each one. The major, natural minor, major and minor pentatonic, as well as the major and minor blues.

Fourth, we have octaves and intervals. These are very important to learn and understand as well because they let us know where the same note is located in different places on the fretboard.

They also allow us to know the distance between notes. This is very helpful in understanding where note location is within certain keys to create chords and scales quicker.

Fifth, we have chord and scale formulas. This where the science of music comes in. By knowing these formulas, we can easily create chords and scales at will. With full understanding of how they work.

Knowing about octaves and intervals is a nice prerequisite for this ability. The ability to find notes and form chords, scales and create the type of emotion as we see fit.

Chapter 8: Additional Training

Lesson 36: Finger exercises

Now we get to the point where we look at additional training. These are a few more concepts and principles that are going to really help you progress as a musician.

The thing we'll look at first is finger exercises. As a guitar player or instrumentalist of any kind, you want to keep your hands and fingers in shape. This can be done with basic stretching of the wrists, and finger exercises.

Exercise #1

Here we start on the 5th fret and use one finger per fret. Index on the 5th, and the pinky on the 8th.

Exercise #2

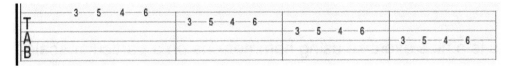

Here we have something similar on the 3rd fret, except the finger pattern changes. This helps with dexterity and finger independence.

130

Exercise #3

A similar concept that starts on the 6th fret.

Exercise #4

Here we do the exercise over two strings.

Exercise #5

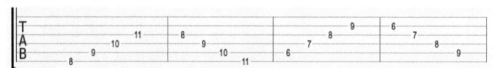

In this example, we exercise across the strings.

Exercise #6

This is a nice exercise using hammer-ons on a particular scale. Can you figure out which one it is?

Study and practice these daily to see some nice improvement in your guitar playing. Then create your own.

Lesson 37: Chord switching

When it comes to playing rhythm, one of the first hurdles to get over is forming guitar chords. The second hurdle to get over is switching between them. In this lesson we'll look at some ways to help you switch chords easier.

The way that I have taught you the chords in this training manual allows for easy switching between them if you learn them in the order I taught. But there will still be times when chord switching can be a bit tricky.

Here are a few tips to help you:

1. Pick two chords that you are having difficulty with and just focus on going back and forth between them. No other chords, just them two. Do this multiple times to get your muscle memory built.

2. Look for ways to reposition your fingers. Many times in songs, if you form chords with certain fingers, it makes it easier to go to the next chord in the progression.

3. Give the muscles in your hands and fingers time to develop. This is a common mistake that beginners make. It is one of the reasons the guitar takes time to play properly.

4. Always be focused on how your hands are forming the guitar chords. Sometimes they seem to have a mind of their own. You must train them to do as you wish.

5. Practice these techniques and your finger exercises daily. It is the only way to get the muscles developed quickly.

Remember, some of these concepts and principles will take time to develop. Everyone learns at a different pace. So take your time to enjoy the journey. Getting there is half the fun.

Do this and I guarantee that it will pay huge dividends in the future.

Lesson 38: Training your ear

One thing about the guitar is that you can play it by ear. This is a very common approach to the instrument. While some people prefer to look at the written word, most guitar players just play by listening and finding the notes on the fretboard.

In fact, there's an old joke that goes, "how do you get a guitar player to turn down?" "You put sheet music in front of him." Try it sometime. See if it works.

But in order to play like this we must train our ears. The best way to do this is to just have the guitar in our hand for 12 hours a day. But of course we can't all do that, so here are some tips to help in this department.

1. Learn the major scale in all 12 keys very, very well. This will help you get familiar with the different tones.

2. Focus on your note intervals. Do you remember what I taught you about note intervals? This can really help you develop your ear.

3. Pick a key and go through the notes on your guitar real slow and try to hum the pitch of each note. This gets the ear familiar with the notes.

4. Play the first note of the scale and then try to match the next note with your voice. Then repeat the process with the next notes.

5. Listen to simple melodies that consist of a few notes and try to find them on the guitar. There are a lot of songs from the early rock n roll era that you can do this with.

6. Listen to the melody and try to find the very first note. Then hum the second one and check if it matches on your guitar.

7. Go through your chords and listen for the notes within each one. Then listen to a simple song and see if you can find the chord progression.

8. Remember, that notes either ascend, or descend along the fretboard. So when finding the interval of notes, in a melody, they can only go one of two ways.

9. Work on your octaves as these will allow your ear to hear a different note pitch, as well as get familiar with note location.

Practice, practice, practice. It is the only way to develop this skill. I guarantee that if you practice 6-7 hours a day, this skill will develop.

Lesson 39: Improvising solos

When it comes to playing guitar solos, the one thing that you want to master is improvising. This is where you put the sheet music away, close all the books and just be one with your guitar.

You just create something on the spot. Just like an improvisational comedian. This can be a bit challenging, but it is a great skill to possess if you ever want to write your own compositions.

Here are a few tips to help you develop this skill:

1. Master your guitar fretboard and be able to hear the pitch of all the notes.

2. Make sure you master your scales and where they are located in each key.

3. Learn guitar solos from your favorite players. This will show you how the techniques we've learned work together in practical application.

4. Study guitar solo phrasing. Remember what this is? Every great lead guitar player has this.

5. Since you know how to read guitar tabs, work at transcribing guitar solos as well as learning them.

6. Use backing tracks (you can find these on YouTube) as a canvas to paint over.

7. Look for ways to incorporate arpeggios, and triads to add different color to your solos.

8. Work on developing a good solid guitar tone. This will inspire you to create.

9. Study different styles of music as these guitar players will all approach soloing differently.

And most importantly, study and practice until you build up your self confidence. Once you do this, you'll be ready to play with other musicians.

Playing music with others can help not just your improvising of guitar solos, but your overall musicianship. Not to mention that if you find the right people it can be a lot of fun.

Lesson 40: Practice habits

Practice habits are what will make all the difference in your guitar accomplishment. It will determine if you become average, or above average. Of course, above average is what we're shooting for right?

Well this all comes down to practice habits. So here are a few that will help you in this area.

1. Create yourself a good solid practice space. A place where you can really focus on your guitar studies. A place that when you go there, your mind will know it's time to practice.

2. Make sure to be organized. Organization is very important for proper progress. If you know where the material is that you're working on, you won't waste time looking for it.

3. Create a good solid practice routine. Most learning can be broken down into two categories. Things known, and things unknown. Work on what's unknown and then finish off the practice with what's known.

4. Always warm up with finger exercises as these will help get and keep your hands and fingers in shape. The better you're in shape, the better you'll be able to execute all the techniques and concepts that you have learned.

5. Study your favorite players. Watch video interviews, read written interviews, and study how they play. They will mention things they do to help them improve and you can use this in your own study and practice.

6. Make sure to take breaks from time to time. This gives the fingers, and mind a chance to recharge. Sometimes when you take a break and come back, it makes more sense.

7. And most of all, have fun in your guitar practice. Because if it's not fun, why do it? Learning guitar should be fun. So make sure this is firmly planted in your mind as you study and practice.

If you take time to study this lesson and put it into action, I guarantee you will become an accomplished guitar player in no time. But in order to do this, you must take learning guitar seriously.

Chapter 8 Summary

In this chapter we have learned some things that can really help you take your guitar playing to the next level. But they must not just be studied, they must be applied. Applied on a daily basis in order to get the most out of them.

Great guitar playing only comes from applying what you have learned on a continuous basis. The ability to be consistent, dedicated, and committed to the cause. If you can do this, you can become a great guitar player.

First, we have finger exercises. These will really help you with all the chords, scales, and techniques you have learned so far. Keeping your hands in shape can make a world of difference.

I recommend you work on these first. Whenever you pick up your guitar to play it, do finger exercises and warm up your muscles. Very much like an athlete. This will also help with injury and fatigue.

Second, you want to focus on chord switching. Some songs stay on chords long enough to form and hold them. But other songs don't. By time you get to the chord, it's time to jump to the next one.

This can be frustrating at first. But if you work on chord switching on a consistent basis, you'll get better at it and these types of songs will become easier to play.

Third, we have ear training. This is a very important skill to develop as it helps you to figure things out better. Study the tips that I have given in the lesson and you'll be well on your way.

Of course this skill can only be developed through having that guitar in your hand as much as possible. Studying the tips and knowing them in theory is not enough, you must put it into practice on a daily basis.

Fourth, we have improvising solos. This can be a lot of fun once you learn to do it properly. Once again, study the tips that I have presented as they will give you a solid foundation of how to improvise.

Like ear training, this must be worked on daily. It is the only way to develop this skill. Just like reading sheet music (or tabs) you've got to work on it daily for it to stick in the mind.

Fifth, we have practice habits. Probably the most important lesson in the whole book. Develop solid practice habits and you will progress faster, accomplish more, and build self confidence.

Learn To Play Electric Guitar Quiz

Last but not least I present you with a simple test. A chance for you to gauge how well you know the lessons taught in the book. Taking a test is a good idea and is presented for you and you alone.

So no need to feel uncomfortable. It's just a way for you to judge for yourself what has stuck in the mind and what hasn't. This is common when introducing new information to the brain. Especially concepts related to music.

So take the test, grade yourself and see what you know, and what you still need to work on. All the answers will be in the lessons themselves. Good luck and have fun.

Q: What are the parts of the electric guitar?

A: _____

Q: What is the best posture for learning the electric guitar?

A: _____

Q: What are the two hand positions?

A: _____

Q: What are ways you can tune the electric guitar?
A: _____

Q: Why use a guitar pick?
A: _____

Q: What is the purpose of the amplifier?
A: _____

Q: What is the purpose of a guitar cable?
A: _____

Q: What are guitar pedals?
A: _____

Q: What's the difference between stomboxes and processors?
A: _____

Q: What is guitar tablature?
A: _____

Q: What are chord charts?
A: _____

Q: What are natural chords?
A: _____

Q: What does it mean to strum chords?

A: _____

Q: What does it mean to arpeggiate chords?

A: _____

Q: What is a chord progression?

A: _____

Q: Why is it important to develop good timing?

A: _____

Q: What is a guitar riff?

A: _____

Q: What does the term lead guitar mean?

A: _____

Q; What is the major scale?

A: _____

Q; what is the natural minor scale?

A: _____

Q: What is the minor pentatonic scale?

A: _____

Q: What is the major pentatonic scale?

A: _____

Q: What is the blues scale?

A: _____

Q: What are hammer-ons & pull-offs?

A: _____

Q: What are bends & slides?

A: _____

Q: What are vibrato & trills?

A: _____

Q: What are the two common types of harmonics?

A: _____

Q: What does the term phrasing mean?

A: _____

Q: Why learn the notes on the guitar fretboard?

A: _____

Q: How are guitar chords created?

A: _____

Q: How are guitar scales created?

A: _____

Q: Why are octaves and intervals important to know?

A: _____

Q: What are chord & scale formulas?

A: _____

Q: Why practice finger exercises?

A: _____

Q: What is one way to switch chords faster?

A: _____

Q: What is one way to help train your ear?

A: _____

Q: What does it mean to improvise a guitar solo?

A: _____

Q: What difference can practice habits make on your playing?

A: _____

146

Learn Electric Guitar Conclusion

If you've made it this far I congratulate you on your efforts and say "thank you for time, and the purchase of this book." You seem like a student that I'd love to teach in person.

This book has taught you many things about the electric guitar. They should now provide you with a basic understanding of concepts and techniques associated with the instrument.

In addition to that, we have touched on some basics of music theory. This can be very beneficial as well as it unlocks some of the mystery of the guitar fretboard.

Along with that, it provides a foundation to build upon for future studies. As time goes on, you want to keep learning. Read more books, watch more videos, and learn from others. The guitar is a great instrument for this. Always more to learn.

No matter if it is guitar chords, strumming patterns, chord progressions, scales, or guitar pedals. There is always more that you can learn. So if you develop a desire to learn, you can keep playing the instrument for years to come.

148

Remember that anything worth doing is worth doing right. So take you time to make this happen. You are learning skills that can last you a lifetime and allow you to pass on to others if you choose to do so as I have done here to you.

Also remember there is always a learning curve with any new type of education. The electric guitar is no different. Just hang in there through the tough times and you will gain confidence in yourself, and come out a winner. I guarantee it.

And if you need additional help with any of the lessons I teach in this book, feel free to shoot me an email through my website at Dwayne's Guitar Lessons and I will be happy to help you.

You can also contact me through any social media avenue as I am on just about everyone of them. It never hurts to reach out for help. That is what I'm here for.

Be sure to visit my website, follow me on Social Media for my latest lesson updates, and subscribe to my Youtube channel.

Keep learning and having fun.

Sincerely, Dwayne Jenkins
Tritone Publishing. copyright © 2020

Other Books By Dwayne's Guitar Lessons

How To Play Guitar Solos

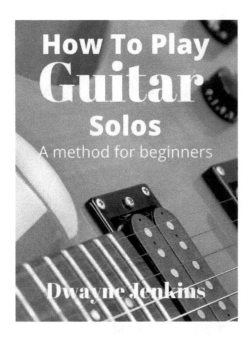

A beginners step-by-step guide to guitar solo basics.

How To Play Guitar Solos will teach you:

1. What scales are most common.
2. Where to find the scales in any key.
3. When to play them within a song
4. Techniques used by all the great guitar players

And many many, more things to help you develop the skill of playing hot guitar solos as a lead guitar player.

Learn To Play Acoustic Guitar

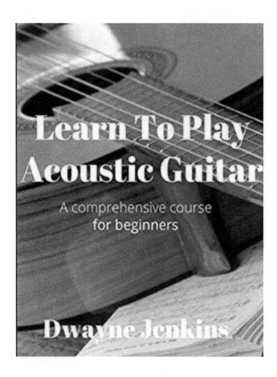

A simple step-by-step study on playing acoustic guitar.

Learn To Play Acoustic Guitar will teach you:

1. What kind of acoustic guitar to purchase
2. How to hold it for best playing results
3. Getting started with your first chords
4. How to read basic sheet music

And many more things that will get you playing the acoustic guitar in no time. A great addition to this book.

These and all other books authored by Dwayne can be purchased through Amazon or Dwayne's eBay store. If purchased at his eBay store, you will receive a "personally signed to you" author copy.

So be sure to check out all guitar books and lessons by Dwayne. You'll be able to take your guitar playing to the next level.

152

Dwayne's Guitar World:

Along with teaching private guitar lessons throughout Denver Colorado and providing training guides, blog posts & videos, Dwayne also has an eBay store to provide you with additional inspiration.

Here you will find guitars, strings, picks, straps, cleaners, rock & roll collectibles, t-shirts and many other items to help you keep your guitar maintained and your skills at peak performance.

And of course the store would not be complete without his very own line of personally branded rock & roll apparel. Such things as guitar picks, t-shirts, baseball hats, beanies & coffee mugs. Which are all designed to provide you with inspiration to keep having fun.

So if you're looking for help in fueling your desire to learn guitar, look no further than Dwayne's Guitar World.

154

About the Author

Dwayne Jenkins is a self accomplished musician and a professional guitar teacher. He has been learning, playing and teaching guitar lessons throughout Denver, CO for almost two decades.

He is now bringing his special training skills and methodology that has been honed and hand-crafted throughout the years on how to play guitar to students around the world.

Dwayne has a unique exciting approach that gets students of all ages and skill levels enjoying the fun of playing guitar. His enthusiasm and love for teaching shine through with every lesson that he creates.

His lessons are designed to enhance your ability to progress. No matter your reason for learning guitar, there will always be something in Dwayne's guitar books and products to help you achieve your dreams.

So if you're a student looking to start, or a student looking to further your education, be sure to get involved with Dwayne's guitar lessons and learn what so many people have already discovered why learning to play guitar is one of the greatest things you can do for yourself.

What Students Are Saying About Dwayne's Guitar Books & Lessons

"The beginners instruction book Learn To Play Guitar Solos by Dwayne Jenkins is an excellent guide for playing lead guitar. It covers everything from scales, to learning to solo. Including ear training and harmonizing. The exercises are fun and make you want to learn more." **Cheryl**

"You really enjoy teaching and you know the fretboard like the back of your hand.I definitely recommend your books, and watching your videos. As always, great job Dwayne."
Mike

"Dwayne, thank you so much for everything you have taught me and done for me. You are an amazing guitarist and wonderful teacher" **BJ**

"Dwayne, thank you for being a great teacher and teaching me many great songs. This is a skill that will last me a lifetime."
Danielle

"I bought your How To Play Guitar Solos book, absolutely phenomenal so far. Was in a rut with my playing recently as I could play decent rhythm but struggled with soloing. Good Job man." **Euan**

"The book Learn To Play Acoustic Guitar is a sure path to learning how to play an acoustic guitar! It will provide a pleasant learning experience as it covers everything a beginner needs to know. The book is straightforward and it is really nice to be able to practice as you read through the lessons, not just read. There are plenty of examples and diagrams to help the reader understand how to play. I also really appreciated that you're given recommendations on what type/brand of equipment is worth looking into for things like guitar picks or a tuner. Lastly I'd like to acknowledge that you're also provided access for personal help, after all, nothing beats an actual teacher! All in all, This is an excellent book to get you started on playing acoustic guitar." **Michelle**

"Dwayne, we want you to know we are honored to have you at the studio. We appreciate all that you do and are grateful that we can leave you in charge" **Angie & Wilson M.E.C**

"Dwayne, we are so glad you are our Teacher. It's been three years already, can you believe it? Thank you again. You're the best!" **Chelsey & Lucas**

"Dwayne, we are so glad that you are in our lives. Chelsey & Lucas really enjoy their time with you, and look up to you. Looking forward to another great year!" Love and best wishes, **Ken & Sue.**

"Dwayne, thank you so much for being not only an awesome guitar teacher, but an awesome friend as well." **Kayla**

"Dwayne, thank you so much for all the years of doing lessons. You have been very patient with my progress and helped me to build confidence in myself and inspired me to follow my dreams. And in doing so you have become a great friend." **Jake**

"Dwayne, Thank you so much for teaching me every Saturday and not only teaching me guitar but also about life and helping me with setting my goals. You are a great teacher, mentor and the best friend ever." **Carson**

"There is not another person I would want to be teaching me guitar! His 1 on 1 teaching makes learning guitar very personal & exhilarating. He teaches at your pace and takes pride in what YOU want to learn. The best part...if Dwayne doesn't know a song a student wants to play, he takes time out the week to learn it. His teaching comes to life in my performance and has progressed over the last 8 years. Words cannot describe how amazing a teacher, rockstar and true friend Dwayne has become to me." **Dominic**

"Dwayne's books are well written and easy to follow. I would definitely recommend his books to anyone wanting to learn guitar. You can easily find them on Amazon." **Betty**

CPSIA information can be obtained
at www.ICGtesting.com
Printed in the USA
BVHW050103020321
601387BV00013B/1190